What Freud Reall

A Chronological Reconstruction of his Theory of the Mind

SUSAN SUGARMAN
Princeton University

CAMBRIDGE
UNIVERSITY PRESS

CAMBRIDGE
UNIVERSITY PRESS

University Printing House, Cambridge CB2 8BS, United Kingdom

Cambridge University Press is part of the University of Cambridge.

It furthers the University's mission by disseminating knowledge in the pursuit of education, learning and research at the highest international levels of excellence.

www.cambridge.org
Information on this title: www.cambridge.org/9781107538559

© Susan Sugarman 2016

First published 2016

Printed in the United Kingdom by Clays, St Ives plc

A catalog record for this publication is available from the British Library

ISBN 978-1-107-11639-9 Hardback
ISBN 978-1-107-53855-9 Paperback

Cambridge University Press has no responsibility for the persistence or accuracy of URLs for external or third-party internet websites referred to in this publication, and does not guarantee that any content on such websites is, or will remain, accurate or appropriate.

What Freud Really Meant

Through an exacting yet accessible reconstruction of eleven of Freud's essential theoretical writings, Susan Sugarman demonstrates that the traditionally received Freud is the diametric opposite of the one evident in the pages of his own works. Whereas Freud's theory of the mind is typically conceived as a catalogue of uninflected concepts and crude reductionism – for instance that we are nothing but our infantile origins or sexual and aggressive instincts – it emerges here as an organic whole built from first principles and developing in sophistication over time. Sugarman's exciting interpretation, tracking Freud's texts in the order in which he wrote them, grounds his claims in the reasoning that led to them and reveals their real intent. This fresh reading will appeal to specialists and students across a variety of disciplines.

SUSAN SUGARMAN, Professor of Psychology at Princeton University, came to the study of Freud as a developmental psychologist who found in Freud's works a striking theory of how the mind develops and a singularly incisive method of argument. She transitioned from studying children in their own right to trying to understand the adult mind by looking for the child within it. A former Fulbright scholar and Guggenheim fellow, she is the author of four other books, including *Piaget's Construction of the Child's Reality* and *Freud on the Psychology of Ordinary Mental Life*.

For Stephen and Abby

Contents

Acknowledgments

What Freud Really Meant grew out of over two decades of my teaching Freud's theory to Princeton University students, whom I thank for their wisdom, open-mindedness, and spirit of adventure. A grant from Princeton generously supported the preparation of the manuscript. Cindy Hyden offered invaluable editorial feedback throughout the drafting process, moving seamlessly between naïve observer searching for clarity and seasoned sleuth ferreting out the merest incongruity. Hetty Marx, Carrie Parkinson, and the staff at Cambridge guided the book to fruition with thoughtfulness and care. To all a heartfelt thank you.

Introduction

Sigmund Freud described as the aim of his life's work to "throw light upon unusual, abnormal or pathological manifestations of the mind" (1936/1981, p. 447). That entailed tracing them back to the psychological forces behind them and discovering the basic mechanisms behind those forces. The general theory of mind he fashioned from that effort attempts no less than the explanation of human mental life from its merest beginnings to the labyrinthine processes capable of producing both mental illness and our highest intellectual and cultural achievements.

Freud has taken his place among the thinkers who have changed our lives. We see human mental life through his idiom. For instance, the conventional wisdom holds that our motives may be other than what they seem, our proclivities may express our early history, and we further our mental health by being aware of our inner longings. But a far more complex and nuanced theory lies behind such virtual commonplaces. Freud's theory is a structure of closely interlocking interdependent parts, whose most fundamental constructs Freud modified, expanding, revising, and incorporating them into an increasingly sophisticated vision.

To know what Freud really meant requires careful tracking of his process and that evolving vision. That tracking is the work of this book. Treating eleven of Freud's essential theoretical writings in chronological sequence, it reveals a systematic structure evolving in complexity over the course of Freud's career. It takes each argument apart and reconstructs it to articulate the theory as perspicuously as possible from the principles Freud designated as foundational.

That foundational understanding is critical to all who would know Freud, from first-time readers to scholars across the many disciplines that study or apply Freud's thought – among them psychology, anthropology, sociology, history, philosophy, literary studies, architecture, and the arts. But as a result of the assimilation of Freud's work by so many fields, it has become fragmented – a concept here, a trope there, claims isolated from their germinating context. Such efforts, in removing the ideas from their original setting, inevitably distort them. We lose sight of what the ideas are as Freud construed them and why he construed them as he did.

By way of example, consider Freud's pleasure principle, the idea that in our doings we strive to avoid pain and where possible cultivate pleasure. The idea at least superficially resembles the Utilitarian objective of happiness, happiness in that tradition encompassing both pleasure and usefulness. Utilitarian thought posits happiness as an ideal, however, a metric toward which we ought to strive, whereas Freud's pleasure principle expresses an observation of a central human tendency (Govrin, 2004). That observation, anchored in a web of considerations tracing all the way back to mere reflexive function, characterizes the most elemental principle to which, according to Freud, our mental life conforms.

The fragmentation of Freud's theory has had the further consequence of affecting the way in which it is understood in the popular and critical imagination – what we might call the culturally received Freud. Freud's ideas are crudely reduced to contending that we are possessed by infantile urges, driven by sex and aggression, and dominated by unbridled hedonism. Although those characterizations do embody constituents of Freud's theory, they communicate only part of it: Freud is trivialized to say we are *nothing but* our infantile origins and sexual and aggressive instincts, and we strive *only* for pleasure. This culturally received Freud is, as the book will show, the diametric opposite of the Freud of the pages of his own works.

The book maps out Freud's master program. It presents his theory as the edifice it is, an explanation, from first principles, of human mental life from its origins to the intricacies of the modern adult mind. Continually evolving entity that it also is, the theory unfolds in layered, overlapping fashion in the target writings, which consist of some of the shorter works that represent identifiable steps in Freud's thinking.

They begin with the 1911 "Formulations regarding two principles of mental functioning" and end with *Civilization and its Discontents*, from 1930. The former introduces his "pleasure" and "reality" principles and the latter integrates these with the later additions and emendations Freud made to the theory. The intervening texts include three of his papers on metapsychology, the endeavor that looks at the mind in self-consciously theoretical terms, and other similarly schematic contributions. In that group are his 1914 paper propounding the concept of narcissism; his speculative *Beyond the Pleasure Principle* of 1920; *The Ego and the Id* (1923), which introduces the hypothetical agencies of "id," "ego," and "superego"; and his short paper on masochism, in which he revises his concept of pleasure and how we pursue it. The book's opening chapter visits Freud's accessible summary of his early theory, *Five Lectures on Psychoanalysis* (1909a). The Epilogue sets the theory into relief against reductive accounts of it.

Freud's works, despite their occasional turgidity and sometimes arcane idiom, are gracefully turned, and they tell a story – a fascinating and resonant one that evokes mental life as we live it and finds its pulse.

I Freud on psychoanalysis: *Five Lectures on Psychoanalysis* (1909a)

> The task is ... to discover, in respect to a senseless idea and a pointless action, the past situation in which the idea was justified and the action served a purpose.
>
> – S. Freud, *Introductory Lectures on Psychoanalysis*, p. 270.

Freud, trained as a medical doctor, turned to psychology after studying treatment of the neurotic disorder hysteria with the French neurologist Jean-Martin Charcot. In the 1890s he collaborated with Viennese physician Josef Breuer in an early improvisation on what would become psychoanalytic treatment of that disorder – one in which patients exhibited behavioral symptoms ranging from tics to severe paralysis, all without organic basis.

His theory originated in that experience and remained accountable to his clinical observations thereafter. In 1909, by invitation of the president of Clark University in Massachusetts, Freud presented some of those observations to a predominantly lay audience. His addresses, published as Five Lectures on Psychoanalysis, *engage both theory and therapy; their ongoing synergy would drive Freud's contribution then and going forward.*

Freud makes the critical point in that slender work that psychopathological symptoms, like more evidently rational behavior, have a sense. They are determined, by which he means they follow coherently from some premise in the person's mind. They serve a purpose. Thus, the human mind, and even the diseased human mind, as Freud conceives it, is not a mad, seething cauldron; it has integrity and structure.

After grounding his conception in an illustration of psychopathology, Freud calls for and proposes a psychological explanation of mental illness. Then, drawing on his clinical experience, he out-lines techniques of psychoanalytic therapy through which he found it possible to uncover the source of individual ailments and cure them. Next he describes a general etiology of disorder that has resulted from his efforts, which brings him to a discussion of what he calls the sexual function and its place in human development. He concludes with an extrapolation to the nature of psychological health.

THE SENSE OF SYMPTOMS AND THEIR IMPLICATIONS
FOR UNCONSCIOUS MENTATION

In his first lecture, Freud discusses a case of hysteria treated by Breuer and draws from its symptoms and treatment a justification of the existence of unconscious mentation. Before Breuer, hysterias, labeled as such by the medical establishment in keeping with the ancient Greek designation, were held to be associated with previous emo-tional shock and were largely dismissed. Breuer, and subsequently Freud, approached sufferers instead with sympathy and interest. They began treating them through the use of a "talking cure," as they called it after a patient's description, in which patients recalled, initially under hypnosis, memories associated with their symptoms.

That patient, known in Freud and Breuer's writings as Anna O., suffered a panoply of symptoms in connection with which she was able to summon fragments of traumatic scenes during which she had originally suppressed powerful affect. For example, when she suffered an inability to drink despite unrelenting thirst, she recalled her revul-sion upon having once caught sight of her governess's detestable dog drinking from a human cup. Although at the time of the encounter she had out of propriety withheld her reaction, she now re-experienced the event with a rush of disgust. She awoke from her hypnotic trance pleading for water, which she immediately drank.

Based on such data, Freud and Breuer concluded that hysterics suffer from unconscious "reminiscences" (p. 16) of traumatic experi-ences. Their symptoms arise as internally coherent, though outwardly maladaptive, overreactions to the memories, occasioned by patients' suppression of powerful affect at the time of the instigating events. Discovery of that pattern provided the grounds for Freud's iconic belief that much of human mentation occurs outside awareness, or unconsciously, and can influence conscious experience and behavior.

THE PSYCHODYNAMIC PERSPECTIVE ON PSYCHOPATHOLOGY

The dominant view of hysteria when Breuer and Freud began their collaboration ascribed the illness to a pervasive degeneracy of the nervous system, which causes the system to abort some of its operations. But a general weakness of that kind, Freud argues in his second lecture, cannot explain the normal and even superior intellectual function exhibited by some sufferers. Anna O., for example, while beset by her symptoms, exhibited heightened fluidity in a foreign language, among other capabilities. Freud, accordingly, believed himself licensed to develop a more specific, psychological hypothesis involving the dynamic interaction of different interests within the mind.

Given that patients could recover otherwise inaccessible memories when under hypnosis, he reasoned, some force must be holding the memories from conscious awareness. He conceived that force as a *resistance* to the material, the resistance driven by interests, like propriety or safety, that lead us to perceive the material as threatening. The effect of that unconscious resistance is the *repression* of the memories, the forcing of them from consciousness.

Freud adduces the case of Elisabeth von R. to further illustrate that dynamic. When under treatment for neurosis, she, like Anna O., recalled a painful memory she had evidently repressed. In the memory, upon arriving at the bedside of a beloved sister who had just died, she had the fleeting thought that the sister's husband, to whom she had felt attracted, would now be free to marry her. She immediately banished the heinous thought, but subsequently developed symptoms – the involuntary production of a clacking noise. Here, then, was a wishful impulse that collided with a competing imperative and was swept from consciousness, in the aftermath of which the patient fell ill. The recall of the impulse restored her health. So again were Freud's thesis about the role of repression in the development of psychopathology, and the effectiveness of "the talking cure" in its elimination, supported.

By the time Freud treated Elisabeth von R., he had abandoned hypnosis as the means by which to elicit unavailable memories from patients. It had proved a temperamental tool, and one to which not all patients responded. It also masks the forces of resistance without eliminating them. Freud observed that in the altered state brought on by hypnosis patients at best momentarily retrieve the repressed material they are after. Once they regain consciousness, their resistances move back into place, ready to repulse disturbing content angling for expression.

Conscious efforts to retrieve the lost content, by contrast, trigger and actually expose the resistances. It is only at that juncture that patients can work to overcome them. The conscious overcoming of the resistances both reveals the forgotten content and disarms the resistances to it, leading to an enduring cure.

Freud remarks, before turning to the question of just how therapy might harness resistances, that symptoms themselves represent a partial failure of repression. Because they express blocked content in disguised form, they circumvent the forces of resistance, as exemplified by Anna O.'s inability to drink. And because that failure represents the repressed material's coming partially forward, it provides a point of departure for the unmasking of additional forbidden material.

THERAPEUTIC TECHNIQUE

How, Freud asks at the start of his third lecture, might therapy seize upon that point of departure to dislodge layers of resistance through conscious dialog and recover the pathogenic formations behind them? One tactic, in which Freud instructed patients either to say the first thing that came into their minds in connection with their situation or to respond to a prompt, met with mixed success at best: the ideas patients generated were too remotely related to the repressed content to help them recover it.

But, Freud realized, holding to his thesis of determinism, that remoteness made them no less suited than patients' more transparent offerings as points of departure in the search for the repressed content. The search would simply require more steps. Accordingly, he made the assumption that any idea patients offer when they are struggling for insight has to have at least some connection to the sought-after material. As their symptoms themselves express, such patients grapple with both concealed impulses striving for expression and equally strong forces of resistance to keep the impulses from awareness: Anna O.'s inability to drink expressed her repressed revulsion at the dog's drinking from a cup *and* served to disguise the disgust. Likewise, intermediate ideas patients might generate about those symptoms would express both.[1]

With respect to the search process in itself, patients could be asked what associations – thoughts, recollections, etc. – a symptom, intermediate idea, or other circumstance evokes. Then they could draw associations to those new associations, under the operating assumption that eventually they would come upon their repressed thoughts.

Freud discovered that for the process to work, patients had to promise complete candor in articulating the thoughts that crossed their minds, including the reprehensible, the silly, and the obscure or incoherent. Those judgments – that an idea is reprehensible, silly, etc. – represent the voice of resistance, which presumably asserts itself just when patients are verging on the material they would rather keep back.

In addition to symptoms, Freud recognized, dream imagery, and also the apparent mental accidents such as slips of the tongue he called *parapraxes*, could be used as starting points for chains of association in psychoanalytic treatment. He believed, based on both self-observation and work with patients, that dreams express disguised wishes and

---

[1] Freud later (e.g., 1918, p. 66) uses the term *compromise formation* to describe this juxtaposition, especially in the case of symptoms.

thus serve as a "royal road" to the unconscious (1900); parapraxes sometimes betray a counterwish to the intention the person is trying to express (1901).

Freud identified one last starting point for exploration in the healing process in patients' *transference* onto the practitioner of their previous significant relationships. Transference is the process whereby patients come to perceive traits in the intentionally neutral practitioner that might or might not exist. Freud inferred the perceptions to be projections of perceived characteristics of people from the patients' pasts. By this primitive, involuntary means, patients "repeat" rather than "remember," their early relationships; the practitioner, in turn, reflects the perceptions back to the patient, enabling investigation of their source.

THE DEVELOPMENT OF THE SEXUAL FUNCTION
AND THE ORIGIN OF NEUROSIS

The preponderance of neuroses Freud treated via the foregoing techniques turned out to trace ultimately to childhood and in particular to impressions from patients' early erotic experience, as manifested in the nuclear family. Freud calls this segment of life the sexual function, the term *sexual* having a broader meaning than its conventional use. Having already made the defining claim that sexuality extends well beyond genital activity (Freud, 1905a), Freud, in the fourth of his *Five Lectures*, examines its early manifestations, which become the core of many later trends.

He earlier marshaled three sources of evidence for the broad reach of sexuality. One is the existence of perversions, in which body parts unrelated to the genitals become capable of sexual arousal to a degree normally reserved for the genitals; sexual foreplay shows this to a lesser degree. The second is homosexuality, in which sexuality operates independently of the reproductive function, and the third, the subject of this lecture, the reality of sexual activity in children.

Regarding the last, Freud expanded on others' observations of children's interest in their genitals, on the physical side, and the formation of romantic attachments among children in the nursery, on the emotional side: with respect to physical sexuality, children attain stimulation he could only describe as sexual, from nonsexual body parts. Regarding emotional life, Freud had begun to uncover in the course of working with patients a whole erotic drama involving children and their parents that incorporates features we ordinarily associate with later erotic life. The early drama includes such staples as the fixation on particular objects, jealousy, feelings of rejection, and their sequelae – the signs, in short, of the *Oedipus complex*.

Freud observed that initially physical sexuality takes the form only of special sensitivities of particular parts of the body, for example the mouth. Children reap special pleasure from the stimulation of these areas and continually seek to re-experience the pleasure. A progression takes place in which different portions of the body replace one another as *erotogenic* zones as children grow older. It normally proceeds from the oral area to the anal and then to the phallic and finally genital, though with overlap among all four. Although the phallic phase, which implicates only the penis, would seem to apply only to boys, Freud believed both girls and boys for a time take interest in the penis in its own right, apart from its genital function. Girls take an interest in the organ as it appears on boys and men or dwell on the clitoris as a reduced version of it, or both.

The proposition that children's first "sexual" pleasures derive from their own bodies – from thumb-sucking and masturbation, for instance – led Freud to call the first period of sexuality *autoerotic*. But children also begin from an early age to derive what Freud judged to be sexual pleasure from actions that incorporate external others, or *objects*. Freud categorized the latter activities as varieties of *instinct* (see Chapter 5 here).

Some sexual instincts, he determined, arise in pairs of opposites, active and passive. He distinguished as most important among them the desire to cause pain, or sadism, and its passive counterpart, the desire to be the object of inflicted pain, or masochism. Also prominent among the instinct pairs are the active and passive desire for looking:

the urge to look at someone is *scopophilia*, which forms, Freud says, the basis of later curiosity; the desire to be looked at is *exhibitionism*, and it forms the basis of theatrical display. Such impulses do not constitute only isolated sidelights of infant life, Freud contends; rather, like sexuality in general, they exist in a continuous developmental line with later, more evolved activity.

The early sexual instincts that do not become integrated into mature sexuality or rechanneled for other purposes, as scopophilia and exhibitionism do for example, normally become subject to repression. Freud maps important sequelae to the repression of, respectively, *coprophilia* – the marked interest in feces and filth – and early erotic ties, from which detachment is a long and complicated process.

Regarding the coprophilic instinct, only the interventions of those around us deter us from acting on the associated impulses and lead us to classify them as "bad." Our response, under the threat of loss of love, is to drive the impulses out of consciousness, in keeping with the aforementioned susceptibility to repression, although we cannot banish them completely. In place of the impulses we evolve shame, disgust, and eventually morality, all of which consist of more than accumulated knowledge and a recipe for behavior. They include an urgency and configuration of feelings that imply a special stake; that stake goes beyond a concern with their content. Similarly, their genesis exceeds mere learned response driven by a fear of the parents (see Chapters 9 and 11 here).

The normal progression of impulses connected to early erotic ties mandates that children develop from seeing their parents as love objects to treating them as models. That transformation forms the basis of every neurosis, as well as of the basis of morality, according to Freud. He examines this claim in his discussion of the Oedipus complex in later works (see Chapters 9 and 11).

Here, in the context of the repression of early sexuality, he goes on to point out that before the process begins, children attempt sexual researches on their own and others' bodies. They abandon this activity as a failure of their ability, again as a result of prohibitions from the outside, to discover all they need to know to make their understanding complete. In consequence, Freud says, children may develop a sense of inadequacy they may carry through life. They may also form incorrect and alarming inferences about some facts, for example the reason girls don't have penises. At the same time, children's frustrated sexual inquiries may find later expression in scientific inquiry, a theme Freud develops in his 1910 essay on Leonardo da Vinci.

PSYCHOLOGICAL HEALTH

In his fifth and final lecture, Freud comes to the question of what constitutes psychological health, prefacing his remarks with a consideration of the nature of psychopathology. He says that people fall ill when they cannot satisfy their erotic needs in reality. That incapacity can occur as a result of either external barriers, such as imposed isolation, or an internal impediment like guilt.

Illness brings about withdrawal from reality and discovery of some means by which to obtain a substitutive satisfaction. A substitutive satisfaction can take the form of a symptom, like compulsive hand-washing, to eradicate what is at its roots the terror of repercussions from the so-called dirty acts of masturbation. In lieu of or as a prelude to a symptom, an inhibition, such as impotence, may arise that allows people to avoid what brings pain, like the lingering terror of repercussions for their sexual precocity in childhood.

The process that produces neuroses has other outcomes as well, including much that is normal and even valuable, like fantasy life and art. For, Freud says, everyone, and not only neurotics, finds reality unsatisfying, given civilization's exacting standards and the resulting repression, and we all attempt to compensate through fantasy, which affords the wish-fulfillment lacking elsewhere.

Against this backdrop, Freud defines as "energetic and successful" those individuals who both allow themselves to fantasize and manage to turn their wishful fantasies into reality to at least some degree (p. 30). For example, they may through their intimate relationships be able to live out their infantile erotic fantasies, or through their work they may achieve a partial satisfaction of the narcissistic need for self-regard that normally pervades early childhood. When people cannot meld fantasy into reality, they withdraw into their fantasy lives. If they retreat too much, they fall ill. Descent into neurosis is their last refuge.

Freud notes in passing that some of these individuals are fortunate enough to engage reality once again by transforming the fantasies into which they have withdrawn into art. They reconnect with reality, and avoid the descent into neurosis, to the extent their creations reach the public sphere.

All told, the energetic and successful person is not the completely satisfied one, because no one achieves complete satisfaction. Nor is it the wholly repressed or otherwise abstemious one, because those individuals would not find happiness either. It is the person who fantasizes up to a point, to compensate for the imperfect life he or she inevitably leads, and who manages to turn some of the fantasy into reality.

Healthy and neurotic people struggle against the same *complexes*, Freud says. Complexes are collections of mostly unconscious, affectively laden ideas people form in reaction to their childhood relationships. They are the unavoidable product of being born human, and they influence all sectors of mental life. Freud maintains that whether the struggle produces health or a neurosis depends on the relative strength of the forces in conflict, inborn dispositions, and accidental experience. A given instinct may be stronger or weaker in one person than in another, or one person may prove constitutionally more resilient than another in the face of similar environmental stresses.

In closing, Freud returns to evidence of our primal sexual impulses, evidence he has obtained by observing the transferences of patients in analysis. The affectionate and hostile impulses we have both felt toward and perceived in our first significant objects become visible in therapeutic settings like Freud's in which the practitioner assumes a relatively passive role. All a patient can do in that setting is project expectations rooted in past relationships onto a new, undefined partner.

Treating the yield of the transference as a fresh specimen of the past, analysts may reveal it to patients to help them recover their long-buried wishes concerning their early relationships. Once patients confront the wishes, whose repression was what precipitated their illness, they have choices: they may renounce the impulses, consciously, as unworthy and unwanted; they may sublimate them, meaning redeploy them to some higher use, or they may opt to embrace them.

2 The pleasure and reality principles: "Formulations regarding two principles in mental functioning" (1911); "The psychology of the dream-processes" from *The Interpretation of Dreams"* (1900)

Psychical activity draws back from any event which might arouse unpleasure

– S. Freud, "Formulations regarding two principles in mental functioning" (p. 219)

Freud's is first and foremost a theory built from first principles. His protracted search for those principles asks no less than what we are fundamentally and which principles of human mental function are sufficiently basic to extend to all human striving. His early psychological conception, presented first in The Interpretation of Dreams *(1900), finds its most succinct expression in his brief "Formulations on two principles in mental functioning" (1911).[1] That essay, amended by a few extracts from* The Interpretation of Dreams, *furnishes a good point of departure for an exploration of the genesis of his views.*

Freud presents an argument in two parts. First he develops his two principles, the first and more elemental of which, the pleasure principle, holds that we seek in all our doings to avoid pain and, where we can, to cultivate pleasure. Accomplishing that aim does

---

[1] Portions of that conception appear earlier, in Freud's (1895) "Project for a scientific psychology," whose physiologically driven basis he later rejected.

*not, however, automatically entail an adaptation to reality; indeed
the shortest and most easily attained routes to pleasure do not take
reality into account at all and may thus ultimately fail. Therefore,
our ability to satisfy our needs mandates a modification of our striving for pleasure, in the form of our accession to the reality principle,
and a major complication of our mental process to accommodate the
modification. The second portion of Freud's argument describes that
accommodation.*

THE PRINCIPLES

Asked to identify the most elemental principle that governs human
mental life, most people might offer one of the following: acting in the
interest of survival; acting to gain control; trying to maintain self-
esteem; inviting the approbation of others; trying to be happy. Yet we
take risks, some of them life-threatening, such as bungee-jumping,
smoking cigarettes, walking tightropes. And we act to lose control,
through drugs or alcohol, for instance. We take actions that undermine
our self-image: we lie, cheat, or take the easy way out and thereby incur
the wrath, rather than the approbation, of others. We suffer, sometimes
intentionally, by reading tragedies and horror stories, for example, or by
sabotaging our chances to attain something we want.

Freud concluded, in his earliest delineation of an organizing
principle of the mind, that we follow the pleasure or pleasure–
unpleasure principle. If the principle operates in all of our mental
life, then even behavior that appears to run directly counter to it
must conform to it in some way. Although in bungee-jumping we
may risk severe injury or worse, we also seek the pleasure of the
thrill of it, just as we may smoke or abuse other substances for the
immediate pleasure the activity brings; or we may engage in these
and other risky or self-destructive actions to punish ourselves, in
answer to our desire to alleviate our guilt. Even nonvoluntary products of the mind align with the pleasure principle: the most horrific
nightmares, for example, fulfill wishes, in that the horror either
expresses a terror at having the wish fulfilled or realizes the need

for punishment for fulfillment of the wish (Freud, 1900, Second Part [*Vol. V, SE,* 556–558]).[2]

Freud contends that our unconscious, which contains what is most primitive in mental life, runs solely on the pleasure principle. It follows that the pleasure principle, as the lone operating modality of the unconscious, encompasses our first and most primitive mode of thought. Subsequently, in addition to its limitless operation in dreams, it surfaces in adult waking life in our tendency to shut out painful impressions (1911, p. 219). Ultimately this tendency drives symptoms. The compulsive hand-washer *must* scrub, for fear of unbearable distress; within the envelope of the symptom, the patient can forestall the distress, by washing.

In each of these cases – in dreams, in the tendency to flee painful impressions, and in symptoms – we turn from reality. The pleasure principle, therefore, disregards reality, and, as Freud observes at the outset of "Two principles . . .," the question arises of how we come to engage it. That story, which resolves with his postulation of the reality principle, unfolds as follows.

The pleasure principle, in this early formulation of Freud's, expresses the most basic function of the nervous system, to discharge stimuli. Stimuli impinge on the body's receptors and create a state of physical tension. Reflexes, such as blinking in response to light, which are the organism's most primitive action, unpremeditatedly discharge the excitation. We thereby relieve the tension, producing a state of "plea-sure," the heightened tension having created "unpleasure," or pain.[3]

When the stimuli emanate from the inside, like hunger for example, no simple action on the organism's part can banish them; Freud calls the inescapable tensions thus produced *needs.* Given that the organism is initially incapable of any action beyond the reflex, the environment provides the necessary satisfactions in the case of

---

[2] See *The Interpretation of Dreams* (1900) for Freud's lengthy analysis of dreaming as wish-fulfillment.

[3] Although Freud eventually modified the coupling of pleasure and stimulus reduction (see Chapters 10 and 11), he continued to accord priority in mental life to the discharge of excitation.

human infants; however, the organism – the baby – knows nothing of the arrangement; it only experiences satisfaction where it once felt pain.

But, Freud (1900, p. 5 65) continues, any need, once having been fulfilled, automatically calls up the "mnemic image," or memory, of its fulfillment the next time the need arises. The experience of the need, combined with the remembered image of its satisfaction, results in an impulse to re-experience the satisfied state. Freud calls that impulse the first embodiment of the *wish*.

We do more than evoke a remembered image, according to Freud. In our theoretically most primitive mental state we reproduce the entire perceptual experience of satisfaction – we hallucinate the satisfaction. The need felt – for satiety or for (what the external observer knows to be) the caregiver's presence, for instance – we immediately evoke it involuntarily, much as a reflex instantly discharges an external stimulus on contact with it.

Hallucination, on this account, is the mental equivalent of the motor reflex: tension rises and is immediately and automatically discharged. It offers the shortest path to the fulfillment of a need and conforms entirely to the pleasure principle, in the ideal observance of which we would admit no pain. Freud saw evidence of the primitiveness of hallucination in its domination of dreams, dreams, as strictly unconscious, exposing our primal mental characteristics.

Hallucination cannot, of course, relieve actual needs. Consider the situation of babies, who, were they only to hallucinate satiety, would sooner or later feel pain they could not ignore.[4] Although initially the supremely attentive environment may anticipate their needs and supply the necessary satisfaction, no caregiver is perfect, and all progressively loosen the symbiotic bond in time.

Thus, babies need to become able to discern when a satisfaction they perceive is not real; they must let in the pain, rather than shutting

---

[4]   They would eventually feel the pain unless sustained by incessant fantasy, as in halluncinatory psychoses and hunger phantasies (Freud, 1900, Second Part, *Vol. VI*, p. 566).

it out by means of what amounts to fantasy, so as to attain lasting and secure satisfaction. Rather than enjoy the pleasure a hallucinated image, for instance of satiety or of the presence of a beloved other, may bring, they must allow themselves to feel the pain the absence of real satisfaction produces. They must allow themselves to feel the hunger or the longing. Then they can recognize the satisfaction's absence and apply themselves to bringing satisfaction about. In this way the "reality" principle is born. When moved by that principle, individuals look not only for pleasure, but for pleasure that is real, even if the process involves admitting pain.

Freud notes that no organism ever in fact observes only the pleasure principle, given the likelihood of the organism's rapid demise were it do so. To run across the street because it feels good might result in our demise by a truck; to hallucinate satiety would leave us to starve. He is describing a theoretical point of origin, approximated, however, by infants in arms whose needs are readily answered by the environment, from which we progressively move away (1911, Note 4, pp. 219–220).[5]

SEQUELAE OF THE REALITY PRINCIPLE

In Freud's telling, the ascension of the reality principle precipitates numerous further transformations. What follows, first, is an effort to change the real circumstances when the wanted satisfaction proves lacking. With this step we make the transition from being the passive recipient of experience to becoming the engineer of it. To take that step we need the mental equipment that will allow us to effect the changes we desire.

The birth of cognitive capability

Historically, Freud surmises, continuing his speculative narrative, that transition would have required the development of sense organs directed toward the outer world. We would have needed

---

[5]   Freud gives an account of primordial reality function in "Instincts and their vicissitudes" (1915a; Chapter 5 here, see under "The impact of instincts" and Note 4).

consciousness to register the qualities of the environment detected by the sense organs in addition to the qualities of pleasure and pain. We also would have had to begin to search the outer world for data we could use to address urgent needs if and when urgent needs arose. *Attention* would have evolved to realize that function. *Memory* would have developed as a system of notation to keep track of the results. In place of the automatic repression of painful impressions there would have arisen the passing of *judgment* on the truth or falsity of ideas, or their agreement with reality; that judgment would have been reached on the basis of a comparison of the impression with memory traces of real conditions.

In conjunction with these various cognitive acquisitions, the function of motor discharge would have changed. Previously, when driven solely by the pleasure principle, motor discharge would have embodied only the reflexive release of accumulations of stimuli, like babies' reflexive crying and thrashing about when they are hungry. Now, in answer to the program of re-finding in reality the satisfaction once achieved there, motor discharge would have become *action* for purposes remembered in advance (Freud, 1911, p. 221).[6] Thus, for example, babies' crying, once they have recognized the need to harness the reality principle, is no longer reflexive, but purposive, the purpose being to signal their desires.

Freud envisions *thought* would have evolved to support the development of action. To repurpose motor discharge for action, we would have needed first to restrain our impulse toward the discharge and then to sustain ourselves through the resulting tension while we chose effective action. Freud describes nascent thought as an experimental way of acting, in which we mentally attempted various maneuvers and, in doing so, occupied the gap between impulse and action. He adds that this way of acting, which we might call a thought-experiment, consumes smaller quantities of energy than full-blown action does. That reduced deployment of energy required the mind to

---

6   In individual development increasingly intentional action develops over the first several months of life (e.g., Piaget, 1936/1952).

bind the energy within it, instead of allowing it to flow freely as it had formerly done. Freud uses the term *binding* to refer to the restriction of the flow of excitations, or energy, within the mind.[7]

The necessary tools in place, the reality principle does not ascend all at once, or ever fully, in mental life. The two principles – pleasure and reality – continue to vie for expression to some extent. Exertions driven by the pleasure principle work toward pleasure and the avoidance of pain; in Freud's terms they aim to fulfill our *wishes*. Our efforts at the behest of the reality principle strive for what is *useful* and safe. For example, we want sole possession of Mother and to eliminate Father, but, wanting his love and protection too and knowing neither parent would condone our assault, we act dutifully. Freud describes some general results of this state of affairs.

Fantasy

First among these consequences is *fantasy* life, the realm of fantasy-creation that begins with children's play and continues as daydreaming. Once we know and follow the dictates of reality, we reserve one area of mental life in which we explicitly liberate ourselves from those constraints and follow the pleasure principle only. Freud attributes the staying power of fantasy life to the "economic" principle of expending the least amount of psychical energy possible. Fantasy accomplishes that saving both in fulfilling our wishes directly and in allowing us to hold fast to sources of pleasure we have enjoyed before. Holding fast to an old pleasure requires less energy than does the erection of a new engagement; for example, we can resurrect the

[7] Binding occurs with the establishment of connections. Initially Freud, in his *Project for a Scientific Psychology* (1895), envisioned those connections as forming between neurons. As he shifted to more purely psychological theorizing, he depicted binding as occurring through the linking of ideas. Ultimately, in the later development of his theory of instincts, Freud extended the idea of binding to life forms themselves: cells bind to form organisms; organisms, to form collections of organisms; collections of organisms, to form collections of the collections, and so on (see Chapters 7 and 11). Regardless of the entities involved, the formation of connections, and corresponding binding of energy, acts to stabilize and thereby preserve the entities.

same fantasied relationship endlessly, even when the object no longer shares our real life.

Sexual vs. ego (self-preservative) strivings

Next is a result of the gradual and uneven ascendency of the reality principle across different areas of mental life: what Freud calls our sexual instincts, which encompass our erotic and sensual strivings, yield to the demands of the reality principle later and more slowly than do what he calls our ego instincts, our impulses for self-preservation.

Initially the sexual instincts seek satisfaction on the subject's own body and therefore lend themselves to immediate gratification. The possibility of immediate gratification, in turn, allows the sexual instincts to escape the frustrations that attend sexual strivings directed toward external objects. Thus, the early, *autoerotic*, sexual instincts, having no need for the external world, can thrive independently of the reality principle.

Domination of the sexual instincts by the pleasure principle continues even after they begin to focus on external objects. That is because their development is interrupted by a period during which erotic interest in the external world recedes once again; Freud calls that period *latency*. He ascribes the loss of interest in external objects to the resolution of the Oedipus complex. At that juncture, according to him, children abandon their erotic pursuit of their parents, having given it up in shame and defeat and repressed their desires (see Chapters 1 and 9).[8]

The delay in the ascension by the sexual instincts to the domain of the reality principle results, Freud reasons, in a close affiliation between them and fantasy. The affiliation takes shape as the withdrawal of erotic interest in external objects makes way for the resumption of autoeroticism. But because children nonetheless recognize a world of external objects, unlike babies in the initial period of

---

[8]   Elsewhere (1930) he adds the extremely speculative notion that historically the glacial epoch disrupted sexual maturation.

autoeroticism, the reanimated autoeroticism of the latency period can take the form of fantasies involving those objects; fantasy otherwise observes the criterion of all autoeroticism of ignoring the real outer world.

The long domination of the pleasure principle over the sexual instincts disposes them to the action of repression. In a life of auto-eroticism and satisfaction by fantasy, Freud explains, gratification is immediate, and any pain connected with arising impulses is promptly eliminated. Repression – of the offending impulse – complements these processes in its elimination of the source of the pain. Like them, it is set in motion by the resolution of the Oedipal period, with the pain, fear, and frustration we want to escape. Freud describes this need of sexual life for immediate gratification and its affiliated susceptibility to repression, or pain aversion, as the "weak spot" in our mental organization (pp. 222–223), making us vulnerable to neurosis.

In connection with the descent into neurosis, Freud notes some people's sexual strivings advance little beyond the autoerotic and fantasy-dominated function of the latency period; hence they advance little beyond the sway of the pleasure principle. Such people might fantasize about entering into relationships, rather than actually being in them, or they might enter into and sustain relationships but in an only desultory way, while fantasizing about others. Neurotic symptoms can develop from the urge to realize those fantasies and the inability to do so. If the fantasies go too far, then the patient becomes progressively less able to manage reality. The ground is then laid for symptoms, because fantasy cannot deliver all the patient needs, and the patient cannot negotiate reality.

By way of expansion of the last possibility, Freud says later in "Two principles ... " that the particular phase at which development derails will determine the form the disorder assumes, should a disorder arise; he thinks all psychopathologies have their roots in a disruption of earlier development. What is important for the shape of the disorder is the patient's level of development in each of the two trajectories – sexual and ego development – and hence the relative progress in these, when the disruption occurs.[9]

Institutions that protect or help us transcend our pleasures

Although the interests of the pleasure and reality principles clash, they ultimately complement one another, the reality principle supporting the pleasure principle. Absent the reality principle, individuals would ignore signs of potential danger in their quest for immediate but only momentary satisfaction. When pleasure is deferred, under the suasion of the estimate of risk demanded by the reality principle, however, it has the potential to become secure and enduring. Nonetheless, Freud thinks, we do not give up our pleasures easily, even the ones doomed to be fragile and short-lived. We appear instead to have evolved various institutions to safeguard them.

Religious myth, with its promise of reward in the afterlife for the renunciation of lusts on earth, compensates for the shift from immediate to deferred gratification demanded by the reality principle. It does not ultimately result in accession to the reality principle, however, given the roots of the myth in illusion. It only softens the pain reality would bring were we to adhere to it.

Art, meanwhile, although most obviously an embodiment of the supremacy of the pleasure principle, manages to combine the pleasure and reality principles and to do so in a unique way. Like fantasy, art arises from the forcing of the drive for pleasure into new channels. Images we deem it inappropriate to bring to fruition in reality we indulge in in a separate sphere – the canvas, the play, the poem, the musical piece. In that rechanneling, art already observes the reality principle in part, given the intentional deflection of the impulse from material realization. Additionally, according to Freud, artists themselves, who have withdrawn into the world of fantasy in the creation of their art, then, via their special gifts, turn their fantasies back *into*

---

[9]   See, for example, Freud's (1913a) "The disposition to obsessional neurosis: A contribution to the problem of choice of neurosis."

reality. The fantasies become goods for others to consume, the gift allowing the creators to produce something the public will be willing to receive. A renowned writer's novel will engage and please a wide audience – our personal daydreams will not (Freud, 1908a).

We have evolved other institutions to facilitate our acceptance of the dictates of the reality principle directly. Education, by our parents as well as by formal schooling, incites us to rise above the urgings of the pleasure principle and sculpt our behavior so it meshes with the outer world. The pursuit and appreciation of science afford an ideal embodiment of the reality principle and corresponding conquest of the pleasure principle, Freud notes, given science's anchor in evidence. It affords pleasure too, though, in the gratification provided by intellectual work.

Pleasure and reality in the unconscious

Having drawn a firm distinction between pleasure- and reality-based functioning, Freud, in closing "Two principles ...," observes that unconscious processes disregard reality entirely. They consist solely of wishful impulses, and the wishes manifest as fulfilled – as they do in hallucinations – regardless of whether they could ever be fulfilled in reality. Dreams, as products of the unconscious, offer, in Freud's view, a particularly clear example of this state of affairs. He arrived at that view, that dreams consist of fulfilled wishes, from analyses of neurotic patients' and some of his own dreams, using dreamers' free associations to the elements of their dream.[10] But, Freud advises, because dreams follow that template, so must attempts to interpret them:

A man who had nursed his father through his long and final illness had the recurring dream that his father was alive again and talking to him as he used to do. At the same time he knew and felt pained that his father was really dead and was unaware that he was. Following the formula that the contents of dreams express something wished for, the idea that the father was dead needs the amendment "as

[10]   Freud outlines the method and its results in detail and with numerous instances in *The Interpretation of Dreams* (1900). See also Chapter 1 here.

the dreamer wished"; so does the idea that the father did not know he was dead. Freud, expanding upon that analysis, proposes as the dream's interpretation that the man felt deeply saddened on learning that he must have desired his father's death, as a release; and he felt horror at the thought of his father's having known of the desire. The dream thus interpreted becomes an expression of the self-reproaches people often experience after the death of a loved one.

3 Ambivalence and the origin of the civilized mind: "Taboo and emotional ambivalence" from *Totem and Taboo* (1913b)

> Conscience is the internal perception of the rejection of a particular wish operating within us.

– S. Freud, *Totem and Taboo*, p. 68

Insofar as we live to satisfy our basic needs, which, as per the pleasure principle, amounts at bottom to reducing the excitation they cause, those needs may come into conflict with each other. Like the incursion of "reality" into the dictates of the pleasure principle, such conflict occasions a major step forward in the development of the mind. This chapter tracks Freud's account of that development in the second chapter of his Totem and Taboo *(1913b) entitled "Taboo and emotional ambivalence."*

In Totem and Taboo, *Freud makes his first attempt to apply the findings of psychoanalysis, which have until then been drawn from the study of individuals, to broader problems of societal life. In this new effort Freud takes the bold step of comparing so-called primitive tribes as known through the work of anthropologists, neurotic individuals of his own culture, and contemporary children.*

Although aware that such parallels as he might observe could prove only superficial, Freud hopes to extrapolate from the cases whose psychology he finds clear to at least a hypothetical psychology of more elusive cases. One striking extrapolation is the insight that the taboo practices of so-called primitive cultures share a strong affinity with the obsessive–compulsive symptoms of modern neurotics. Both express ambivalence in their betrayal of contrary attitudes toward the same entity, for example love and hate toward the same

object or temptation toward and dread of committing the same act.
Both embody attempts to mitigate the ambivalence.

A creature able to become disturbed, even unawares, by
contrary attitudes toward the same thing has already advanced
beyond one who only feels pleasure and pain and approaches or
withdraws from the source accordingly. To adopt a compensatory
measure signals a further step. Thus, Freud speculates that the
capacity for ambivalence prompted a further signature advance
in the mind and, as such, lay the basis for the possibility of
civilized life. The chapter will follow Freud's discussion leading
to these points.

TABOOS AS CONVENTIONALLY UNDERSTOOD

Taboos, unlike totemism, the other subject of *Totem and Taboo*, persist to this day, where we may observe them most easily in obsessive–
compulsive symptoms. They are recognizable by their compulsory
nature – a person *must* observe the prescribed practice or frightful
consequences will follow – and the lack of an evident basis for them
(Freud, 1913b, p. xiv). For example, not only must compulsive hand-
washers wash, ostensibly for fear of contamination, they must wash to
such an extent that a dispassionate observer can only doubt the
hygienic motive; the real genesis remains obscure.

The word "taboo" expresses two seemingly contradictory meanings in the original Polynesian, "sacred" and "unclean" (Freud, 1913b,
p. 18). The meanings converge in the idea that the object or act people
are trying to avoid is unapproachable or prohibited. A king may not be
touched because he is sacred. The warrior who slayed an enemy may
not be approached, because he is tainted by the killing.

Freud follows anthropological writers before him this far. They,
however, exemplified by Wilhelm Wundt (1906, pp. 301–313; discussed in Freud, 1913b, pp. 23–25) go on to ascribe these and all
taboo practices ultimately to a fear of demons, whereas Freud believes
veneration (of the sacred) and horror (of the unclean) are unlikely to
have shared a common origin. Moreover, he points out (p. 25) that the

fear of demons cannot have furnished the original source of taboo because demons are themselves creations of the human mind. They do not exist in reality, so the mind must have made them up; if the mind made them up, it made them up out of something – other than the real perception of them. Thus, the source of taboo must lie elsewhere.

TABOO AS ILLUMINATED BY PSYCHOANALYSIS

Freud turns to psychoanalysis for fresh hypotheses about the basis of taboo in the light of the striking resemblance between taboo prohibitions and obsessional symptoms. Both involve a strict avoidance of contact with given objects, persons, words or names, or even thoughts. Both lack any evident motive and have an obscure origin. They persist on account of the uncompromising fear of disaster that would arise if their adherents did not follow their dictates. Each, in addition, is liable to displacement as the danger associated with the initial target of the prohibition spreads from one target to the next until a whole web of associated people and things becomes proscribed.

Freud offers as an example of the process of displacement the machinations of an obsessional patient who insisted her husband get rid of an article he had bought in a shop on a street bearing the same name as a childhood friend of hers. The friend had some time ago become "impossible," that is, taboo, in the patient's mind – not to be thought of, remarked upon, or dealt with – because the thought of her evoked some disturbing association. By extension, an article linked to the friend even through an accidental association became taboo as well.

Thus, Freud summarizes, taboo practices and obsessional symptoms converge on four points: they lack an evident motive; they are driven internally and sustained by fear; they are readily displaced onto new objects; and they materialize into compulsory ceremonial acts (e.g., in obsessional cases, hand-washing) aimed at staving off disaster.

Drawing on case histories of patients with obsessional neurosis treated through psychoanalysis, Freud traces the individual origins of the disease; he goes back to the conflicted feelings that arise in early childhood regarding the touching of our genitals, which typically encounters forceful prohibition. Out of fear of the loss of parental love, children deny the urge to touch, itself strong, resulting in what Freud terms a phobia against *touching* (Freud, 1913b, p. 29). However, on account of the weakness of their still-developing minds, children cannot eliminate the urge. They can only repress it, with the consequence that it persists unconsciously, as does the prohibition against it; without the prohibition the urge would force its way back into conscious operation. The conflict, unresolved, remains, and has the power to influence the mind's operation.

Specifically, people form an attitude of *ambivalence* toward the proscribed act: they want to perform it, and they also detest it. The conflict admits of no solution because its poles exist in separate parts of the mind: the original urge persists unconsciously, and the idea of prohibition – the sense that they must not do, or must avoid, something – persists consciously. The imperatives to wash their hands or to avoid any object or locale associated with somebody's name give conscious expression to the idea of avoiding something, while the real reason for the imperative remains mysterious, because it is unconscious.

Thus, sufferers cannot stop (compulsively) washing their hands, for example, not because the threat of infection always looms, but because they did something "dirty" a long time ago, as a result of which they were threatened with unbearable repercussions from their parents. The threat of infection *does* loom, but normal hygiene is adequate to allay the threat as far as it can be allayed, thus raising doubt about the apparent source of the symptom. The aim of psychoanalytic therapy is to cut beneath this veneer to the real source of the symptom and thereby eliminate the symptom.

But, Freud elaborates, the elusiveness of the original urge – presumably to masturbate in this case – combined with the strength it gained as a result of its being unconscious, complicate this task. Indeed, the same factors, the elusiveness and the resultant strength of the original urge, confer upon the need to prohibit the urge its strength and obsessive quality. The urge, in its constant quest for fulfillment, shifts from one target to another, and the drive to stop it follows it there. The tension between the urge and the drive to stop it presses for discharge. Freud surmises the obsessive acts associated with the neurosis, for example hand-washing, arise to fill this need.

APPLICATION OF THE ANALOGY BETWEEN NEUROSIS AND TABOO

Applying this picture to cultural taboos, Freud hypothesizes that taboos are aimed to check acts toward which people have, and have had across generations, a strong inclination – acts society energetically forbids. Here too the urge exists in the unconscious, and only the taboo against it is recognized consciously.

Taboos, Freud supposes, derive from prohibitions originally forcibly imposed by an external authority against the most powerful human longings, which persisted, and persist, despite the energetic reaction against them. As is true in the case of neuroses, both the desires and their prohibition persist unconsciously and engender an analogous ambivalence. People long to commit the deed, and they despise it. This is Freud's fundamental thesis that emotional ambivalence underlies all of taboo and, by extension, is a major force in our emotional life. The prohibition finds conscious expression in a taboo, which at the same time evokes the forbidden wish unconsciously and, also unconsciously, arouses the temptation to violate the prohibition against it. But the temptation arouses fear of violating the prohibition, the fear made all the stronger by the strength of the temptation. The fear of violation prevails, and results in the immobilization of the individual against the temptation.

To explore this hypothesis, that taboos, like neuroses, consist of compulsive actions driven by ambivalence toward an unconscious urge, Freud examines three classes of taboo documented by the Scottish social anthropologist James G. Frazer (1911a, 1911b): taboos attaching to the treatment of enemies, those concerned with rulers, and those upon the dead. Each of these targets represents a temptation. Enemies evoke the opportunity to act on murderous impulses and rulers evoke the envy of their powers and privileges. The dead elicit the desire to exploit them by virtue of their helplessness, or, as Freud will elaborate in the material covered here, their capacity, in the case of deceased loved ones, to call up hostile impulses against them from the past. Each taboo therefore affords an opportunity for signs of the temptation *and* of a countermovement to surface, which is indeed what Freud finds, in support of his thesis that ambivalence undergirds taboo.

In even the most savage act so-called primitive peoples may commit against enemies, namely killing, a number of taboos attach to the deed that express something less than uncompromising cruelty. The moderation betokens an ambivalence toward the deed. Such taboos include appeasement of the victim, restrictions on the move-ments of the slayer, acts of expiation and purification the slayer must undertake, and various ceremonial rites (Freud, 1913b, p. 37). On the island of Timor in the Malay Archipelago, for example, warring expe-ditions that returned victorious with the heads of slain foes offered sacrifices to placate the souls of the slain, whom they also entreated for forgiveness.

Freud acknowledges the possible objection that these rites may derive from superstition rather than ambivalence, answering a fear of revenge on the part of the ghosts of the slain, for example. This fear was pervasive among the peoples Frazer observed, as well as in anti-quity. Granting the likely contribution of this thinking to the taboos concerning enemies, Freud wants at this juncture to make a more basic point. It is the observation that the attitude toward enemies, who by rights would be expected to enlist people's deepest animosity, is not wholly hostile. Regardless of its source, the attitude mixes with expressions of remorse, admiration for the departed, and pangs of bad conscience. It is ambivalent.

Freud notes rulers submit to restrictions and ceremonials imposed by their subjects that suggest disparagement of and outright hostility toward them, along with the deference and admiration we would expect. Taboos designed to protect rulers, hardly a source of dignity or comfort, constrain their every act and obliterate their freedom (Frazer 1911b, 7f; Freud, 1913b, pp. 43–44). One of the most severe rituals of this kind attended the Mikado of Japan in earlier centuries. To go anywhere, he had to be carried so his feet would not need to touch the ground. He was kept indoors, because the sun was considered unworthy to shine on him. In still earlier times he had to sit motionless on the throne for hours every morning so as to preserve the peace of the kingdom (Frazer, 1911b, 3f, after Kaempfer, 1727, Vol. 1, p. 150; Freud, 1913b, pp. 44–45).

Were the excessive solicitude suggested by these taboos to manifest as a symptom in modern neurotics, it would arouse the attention of the psychoanalyst, Freud observes. Just as symptoms have a sense (see Chapter 1 here), the analyst would surmise, some justification must exist for protective measures that exceed the precautions warranted by objective threats to the leader. In the case of neurotics, such undue solicitude, for example in an interpersonal relationship, would normally signal an unconscious hostility for which they experience the unconscious imperative to compensate. The much-intensified affection shouts down the hostility and becomes compulsive, so as to mask the hostility and restrain it. Because the extreme solicitude shown toward rulers similarly betrays an undercurrent of hostility, the relationship of subject to ruler is ambivalent, consisting of veneration intertwined with animus.

Freud observes that taboos upon the dead treat the dead as enemies. The dead, or their ghosts, rather than incurring love or admiration, are feared. Freud remarks the special virulence of those taboos. They apply to anyone and anything connected with the deceased, including those who mourn them and anything with which the mourners come into contact. Names of the dead are also taboo.

Freud asks why so severe a set of taboos surrounds contact, in any form, with the dead. Obvious explanations would point to the horror aroused by dead bodies and the pain of mourning that follows upon a death. Skeptical of those ideas, Freud notes that horror at the corpse would not account for all the details of the taboos followers observe. Why avoid the name of the deceased long after the corpse has been dispatched? And mourning, although painful, focuses attention exactly on the dead, whose memory it strives to keep alive as long as possible. Mourning, therefore, would not be the agent of avoidance of the dead.

The groups that observe the taboos attest to a fear of the ghosts of the deceased, which they think harbor a murderous grudge against the living and believe can be restrained if the appropriate observances are followed. Granted Freud's position that this explanation cannot be primary because ghosts do not exist, he makes a more fundamental observation here: it is not given that people's loved ones would change upon death into something hostile against which they would need vigorously to defend themselves. As Freud argues in what follows, the hostility actually lies, as it does in the taboos on enemies and rulers, in the observer of the taboo, only in the case of the taboo upon the dead it exists at a greater remove from ostensive behavior. His analysis in that case, although thereby more speculative than the first two analyses, merits attention because it both supports the derivation of taboos from ambivalence and connects with his thinking about ambivalence in modern life.

Freud offers an account of the taboo upon the dead drawn from the analysis of psychoneurotic disorders. Often the passing of a loved one leaves a person's survivors with obsessive self-reproaches to the effect that the survivors precipitated the death through some failing on their part. Analysis shows the reproaches to have had some justification in unconscious promptings that, if not outright wishes for the death, at least would not have found it objectionable. Freud extrapolates the generalization that every intense love is accompanied by an unconscious hostility, and then that this ambivalent disposition exists in everyone and permeates all close relationships; in obsessional neurotics the self-reproachful ambivalence can take a particularly pronounced form after a death.

Freud, generalizing, imagines that primitive peoples or their forebears likewise harbored intense emotional ambivalence – thus both love and hostility – toward their loved ones. Death would provide the ultimate satisfaction of the hostile impulses, for the object is eradicated. But now the affectionate impulses, deprived of their object, cannot discharge; they have no target.

The affectionate impulses therefore constantly accrue, producing the pain experienced as mourning[1] and grow ever more intolerant of hostile impulses, eventually blocking them from realizing satisfaction. As a result, in obsessional neurosis or primitive mentality, where emotional ambivalence is intense, the hostile impulses, unconscious, are projected onto the outside, in the form of looming danger in the case of neurotics and demons in the case of primitive peoples. It is the fears evoked in both cases that give rise to the host of ceremonials and restrictions associated with taboos, or with symptoms.

Thus, both taboos and neurotic symptoms betray the emotional ambivalence they are meant to conceal. They bear the mark of affection, as seen, for example, in mourning or other solicitous attitudes, and they express the original hostility against the loved one. Regarding the latter, the primitives contending with ghosts drive away the now-loathsome enemy; the driving away of something in itself suggests hatred and aggression. The evil intent attributed to the ghost through projection attests to yet another layer of hostility. The obsessive self-reproaches of modern neurotics likewise betray previous death-wishes against the now-deceased, for whom the afflicted also feel affection.

This perspective on the role of taboo and specifically its essential meaning – that something we want to touch must not be touched (Freud, 1913b, pp. 66–67) – supports Freud's evolving belief that emotional ambivalence underlies all human relationships. The account as applied specifically to the taboo upon the dead retains the centrality of the fear of demons argued by Wundt. At the same time it demonstrates

---

[1]   See Freud, 1926, Addendum C, for a later elaboration.

the derivation of demons from more primary psychological forces (see earlier this chapter under "Taboos as conventionally understood"). Additionally the account contests Wundt's (1906) claim that taboo originally had a single meaning: connected with the fear of demons and hence the untouchable, the meaning, on that view, only later split into the two implications of untouchable – sacred and unclean. On the grounds that taboos arose to relieve emotional conflict, Freud suggests the word *taboo* carried the ambivalent meaning – beloved and despised – from the start.

CONSCIENCE: AN ADVANCE IN THE MIND

Freud believes his account of taboo allows an extrapolation to the nature and origin of *conscience*. Taboos, he thinks, represent an exteriorized form of what we now call conscience. They mark that which one must most certainly do, or not do. And they mark it without recourse to reasons; people do not know why they must follow the taboo, only that they must follow it or frightful consequences will occur. Freud has determined that the reasons, in the form of the original forbidden urge, are not accessible to consciousness. The unconsciousness of the originating urge is what makes the compensatory measures undertaken to pursue it compulsive. Corresponding to this earliest form of conscience is a taboo sense of *guilt*, the expectation of certain retribution people would feel – again automatically and without recourse to reason – after having actually violated a taboo.

Freud builds from this prototype and the close connection between the words for "conscious" and "conscience" in his definition of conscience as we know it today. He conceives conscience as our rejection of a wish: we have an impulse toward doing something and have an energetic reaction against doing it. The rejection is "'certain of itself'" (Freud, 1913b, p. 68); it has no need of justification. Similarly, when we experience guilt for a wish we have acted upon rather than rejected, our conviction of wrongness and attendant self-reproaches are unmediated by recourse to reasons.

Obsessional neurotics have developed a severe conscientiousness, or conscience, which, when analyzed, appears to serve as a barrier against an unconscious temptation. Such conscientiousness eventually escalates into a consuming sense of guilt. Freud surmises from that guilt, its analysis, and the absence of any evident wrongdoing, that the strict and inscrutable prohibitions represented by taboos also developed in order to block desires to do the opposite. They blocked the desire to murder rulers, abuse the dead, and so forth. The same would follow regarding our own moral injunctions, for example against killing and incest: we would have no reason to maintain them unless we harbored the temptation to do what they prohibit.

Fundamental to the ambivalence underlying these practices – ambivalence being the source of taboo and, in turn, of conscience – is unawareness of the desire to do what the prohibition forbids. Unconscious impulses enjoy liberties not available to conscious processes. They can move toward people and circumstances other than those to whom and to which they were originally directed. A compulsive hand-washer's ostensible fear of contamination by bacteria might trace to an ambivalent attitude toward committing a dirty act himself – with his hands. This alteration, known as *displacement*, is characteristic of dream and symptom formation, both of which arise from the clash between unconscious impulses and conscious mentation. Freud suggests, extending that idea, that primitives' taboos might likewise, through the displacement of rejected and consequently unconscious impulses, have eventuated in practices remote from the taboos' origin.

Although Freud subsequently refined and elaborated his views of the genesis of conscience (Freud, 1923; see Chapter 9 here), the central point he makes at this early stage still stands. Embodied within taboos, moral prohibitions, the ceremonials of obsessional neurosis, and the ambivalence to which all these forms attest, is an advance in civilization, in the rejection of a wish. To repel an impulse, even unawares, with a taboo or with a symptom, is to do more than wish and act on wishes. It is to rise above the wish, or the urge, which only seeks discharge, and judge and if necessary deny it, again even if only unawares.

Freud already put us on the alert to this type of advance with his (1911) postulation of the reality principle. When guided by the reality principle, according to that sketch, we inhibit an impulse on the grounds that it will not in the end produce the satisfaction we want; we instead endure the discomfort bound to arise from deferring our satisfaction.

But when we reject a wish as a result of the ambivalence we feel toward its satisfaction, we do more than inhibit an inadequate solution. We experience a change in the value of the original impulse on account of a competing imperative we also feel; it is in light of that imperative that we inhibit the original one. The possibility that the process might result in interminable conflict between the two impulses, as it does in the case of obsessional neurosis, in no way diminishes the advance the process represents.

4 Narcissism as a stage in development: "On narcissism: an introduction" (1914)

> It is expedient and indeed indispensable to insert a third stage between [autoeroticism and object-love]. [In it] the hitherto isolated sexual instincts have already come together into a single whole and have also found an object. But this object is not an external one . . . it is [the subject's] own ego.
>
> – S. Freud, *Totem and Taboo*, 1913b, pp. 88–89.

This revolutionary paper of Freud's both identifies a crucial stratum of human psychology – narcissism – and makes far-reaching and compelling claims about the relationship between that trait and other constituents of our mental life. The paper ranges widely in the process, anticipating many later developments of the theory, such as the formation of a superego. Although a bit unwieldy on that account, it compels our attention for those anticipations as well as for its introduction of a novel and critical concept.

Our emotional lives are formed and sustained by our relationships with other people. Primary among these relationships are those with the people we love, our love objects; initially these are our parents or other caregivers. We enter into these relationships from birth, though at first experience only the conglomerate of impressions we will later come to know as self, other, and what happens between them.

Love, in Freud's conceptualization, is a constituent of the sexual instincts. The sexual instincts operate from birth and ultimately organize around reproduction, but, as we saw in Chapter 1, they pass through a number of transitional phases before reaching that point. Freud terms our earliest sexuality autoerotic, in its striving for the attainment of various kinds of pleasure on the body, independent of any external object. Narcissism surfaces as a first integration of the sexual instincts, in which we take ourselves, rather than an external other, as love object. An object relations stage follows whereby sexual activities do assume an external object.

First Freud identifies narcissism as both a disposition in human mental life and a phase in development. He next illustrates the condition via examples from pathology and normal life. He concludes with a case for the continuation of narcissism in our attitude toward what he here calls the ego-ideal and in later writings, the superego.

NARCISSISM DEFINED

The term "narcissism" derives from the myth of Narcissus, who fell in love with his own reflected image. Clinical use of the term originated with its application to people who derive sexual satisfaction, in the extreme complete satisfaction, from the contemplation and manipulation of their own bodies. Freud, among others, recognized in patients suffering from a variety of disorders, and to some degree in all people, a characteristic "narcissistic attitude" (Freud, 1914, p. 65) that goes beyond sexual behavior.

He finds an especially clear manifestation of the broader narcissistic attitude in those people with schizophrenia who exhibit, among other traits, a withdrawal of all interest, including all erotic interest, in the external world. They, by contrast with neurotic people like hysterics or individuals with obsessive–compulsive disorder, abandon their love objects even in fantasy; although some neurotics may cease to pursue their objects in reality, they do engage versions of them in fantasy. People with schizophrenia manifest only self-directed interest, in the form of megalomania or self-aggrandizement. Because that inflation of the ego coincides with the abandonment of any interest directed toward objects, Freud surmises withdrawal of the libido from external objects results in its redirection onto the ego. The directing of libido to the ego is narcissism.

But, he continues, the evident narcissism of schizophrenia must embody a reanimation of an earlier state. The reason is that, as his clinical experience has shown, all nervous disorders, including both neuroses and psychoses, are inherently regressive: they depend on a return of the ego to an earlier level of functioning. The ego regresses in those states as a defensive measure against its unsupportable existence in the current reality.

Freud sees evidence of the state to which the overextended ego of schizophrenics may have regressed in the mental life of children and primitive peoples (Freud, 1914, p. 75). Those groups act as though their wishes, utterances, and other mental acts can influence distal events. They might, for instance, attribute the harm that befalls someone else to an evil thought they had about the person, or they might carry out magical practices, like a rain dance, designed to bring about a desired, distal outcome.[1] Those beliefs and practices contain an overestimation of one's mental powers and thus, like schizophrenic symptoms, can be described as megalomaniacal (Freud, 1914, p. 75). Hence Freud infers an affinity between the two and reasons that schizophrenics have reverted to the narcissistic condition of young children.

A primordial form of narcissism is manifest in babies' incapacity to distinguish the person who feeds them from the comfort of being fed and coddled. Existing in a near-perfect symbiosis with the mother (Freud, 1911, Note 4, pp. 219–220; Chapter 2 here) whereby their needs are met more or less immediately and constantly, babies experience an undifferentiated narcissism. That early narcissism leaves a permanent impress on all people.

Freud finds narcissism an elusive subject to study directly. Because it manifests most clearly in schizophrenia, which so grossly exaggerates the ego's claims, Freud determined that focus on that disorder would provide the clearest view of narcissism and a basis for developing an account of "the psychology of the ego" (1914, p. 82). By that Freud means, in keeping with the direction of the next part of his essay, the way the ego comes to be infused with libido. As

---

[1] Freud details examples in the third chapter of his *Totem and Taboo* (1913b), "Animism, magic, and the omnipotence of thoughts."

he shows next, other less dramatic contexts than a full psychosis like schizophrenia seem also to impact our distribution of libido and hence to expose narcissism.

THREE WINDOWS ON NARCISSISM

Living with physical illness or injury is one such less dramatic context: so long as people suffer, they lose interest in the external world, including their love objects, and indeed cease to love, Freud says (Freud, 1914, p. 82). Once recovered, they love again.

The discomfort induced by hypochondria, an altered mood resulting from an imaginary organic ailment, mimics the physical pain of material ailment and thus engenders the same withdrawal from the outside world as a material ailment does. Sufferers of either condition concentrate on the impacted organ. Although hypochondria lacks an organic base, Freud believes some degree of sexual excitation occurs in the sensation of all pain, whether real or imagined. Thus, alongside the pain hypochondriacs feel, they experience the state of sexual arousal the (pseudo)pain brings (1914, p. 84; see also Freud, 1924, discussed in Chapter 10 here). The interior focus of that arousal leaves less sexual energy available to be directed to the external world; hence the narcissism of hypochondria. Nonetheless, Freud suggests, should we manage to fall in love again, we may recover from the hypochondria.

Love for another offers a third context for examining narcissism, and Freud distinguishes between two types, emphasizing that we rarely assume one exclusively. One, which he calls *anaclytic*, is love in the image of the parents, whereby people seek an object patterned after those who saw to their basic needs in infancy. The other, which is rooted in love for oneself, and which he therefore labels *narcissistic*, arises when people find objects in their own image – objects who represent who they once were or now are or wish they could become. Freud extends the concept of narcissistic love (of another) to parental love, which, insofar as our children are extensions of us, can answer our narcissistic needs.

NARCISSISM AND THE "EGO-IDEAL"

Freud turns in the final section of his essay to a normal manifestation of narcissism carried over and perpetuated into adulthood. This is an aspect of mind Freud terms the *ego-ideal* as of this (Freud, 1914) writing but will eventually call the superego (Freud, 1923; Chapter 9 here). It arises from our internalization of standards against which to measure ourselves. We erect those standards when we come to recognize and accept the imperfections of the ego, which shrinks as we become alert to the admonitions of others, and our own critical judgment awakens (Freud, 1914, p. 94). In thus creating an ego-ideal for ourselves to compensate for the ego's shortcomings, we strive once again for the "narcissistic perfection" of childhood (Freud, 1914, p. 94) and provide an avenue for our self-love to continue. Freud further imagines we form a special agency designed to assure our attainment of narcissistic satisfaction from the ego-ideal. That agency, our conscience, watches over the ego and measures it against the ideal.[2]

Freud notes, in support of this conception, that the childhood characteristics on the basis of which one can infer the existence of infantile narcissism gradually diminish. He wonders whether this means narcissism as a whole, which presumably animated those characteristics, has also receded, in favor of a new interest in external objects. But, although we may become more interested in external objects, he observes, we rarely willingly abandon a libido position – a love object, a pleasure once enjoyed (Freud, 1914, p. 94), or, for that matter anything (Freud, 1908a, p. 145).

Thus, he surmises, in this case as well not all of the libido – the sexual energy – housed in the narcissistic ego gets redirected to an interest in others; indeed, he remarks later in the paper, although the development of our ego wrests us ever further from our primary narcissism, we spend the rest of our lives in a vigorous attempt to regain it. Some libido, he continues in the present instance, must

---

[2]   The superego Freud delineates later (see Chapter 9) encompasses both this watching-over function, or the conscience, and the ego-ideal itself.

remain directed to the ego, but it may do so in a more subtle form than the original one, the formation of the ego-ideal providing a fitting venue.

Freud extrapolates to this new allocation of libido, which is to say to the formation of an ego-ideal, from a consideration of the already-documented psychology of repression (Freud, 1909a); repression is the reflexive withdrawal of consciousness from any instinctual impulse people perceive to conflict with their cultural and ethical standards.[3] For a process depending on that conflict to proceed, people must harbor within themselves the standards to which they will submit unthinkingly. Those standards and the compulsion to adhere to them make up the ego-ideal and conscience, respectively.

Freud identifies an extreme version of this internal process of judgment in the disorder paranoia, or the delusion of being watched and persecuted. The delusion, Freud suggests, represents the reality everyone experiences of being watched and judged by the agency – here conscience – that measures the ego against the ego-ideal. Analysis of the disorder points to a derivation of watching and judging from criticism leveled by the parents and later other authority figures and peers. Paranoiacs want to free themselves from that burden, but rather than disappearing, it confronts them again as a hostile influence from the outside. The impression of an external observer and judge, clearly a projection of internal content, supports Freud's contention that we form an agency that carries out these operations from within.

NARCISSISM AND SELF-REGARD

Freud, having noted a trade-off between narcissism and object-directed love and hence a justification for distinguishing narcissism within libidinal life, turns, in some parting remarks, to further instances of the trade-off.

He points, for example, to *self-regard* as it manifests in both normal and neurotic people. People's self-regard increases with all

---

[3]   See Chapter 6 for Freud's subsequent detailed elaboration.

they achieve or acquire, buttressed by all the vestiges of childhood omnipotence their later experience has seemed to affirm. It satisfies the narcissistic trends that remain within them. Freud cites two trends from pathology in support of that surmise: schizophrenics experience an increase in their self-regard at the same time that they abandon the world of external objects, and the libido they would normally have invested in them flows back to the ego, producing a narcissistic state. Conversely, self-regard is profoundly diminished in sufferers of transference neurosis, who invest libido mightily in objects that seem to elude them; loving by itself, absent its return, depletes, rather than reinforces, the ego.

5 The impetus to the mind: "Instincts and their vicissitudes" (1915a)

Instincts and not external stimuli are the true motive forces behind the advances that have led the nervous system, with its unlimited capacities, to its present high level of development.

– S. Freud, "Instincts and their vicissitudes," 1915a, p. 120

This paper establishes the force that prods the psychical system to action, which is to say the occurrence that produces the tension due to need, such that the organism undertakes to dispel the tension. That force is the impingement of stimuli, which divide into excitations arriving from without, like a bright light striking the eye, on the one hand, and those, like hunger, on the other, arising from within. Freud calls the latter group instincts. Instinctual needs, so defined, provide an especially potent impetus to the system because of the complexities involved in satisfying them. Although we can flee an external stimulus, we cannot escape an internal one, such as the pain of hunger. We have to satisfy it.

The paper also contains Freud's first pass at categorizing the possible instincts that can arise. In this effort he strives to distinguish those instincts that are so basic they admit of no further analysis. He selects for the purpose the ego and sexual instincts, drawing from the prototype of hunger and love. The ego instincts address self-preservation, and the sexual instincts a range of interests extending from the production of pleasurable sensations on the body to our emotional connection with others. The two classes of instincts also express the distinction between individual and species continuity. The ego instincts preserve the individual, and the sexual instincts the species.

Freud next develops his theory of how instincts function based on the sexual ones, which he finds the easier of the two classes to observe. Accordingly, the final section of the paper addresses the continuity that exists across at least the part of our mental life occupied by the sexual instincts and their derivatives. In what Freud will label "vicissitudes," these instincts can transform one into the other, for instance the instinct of sadism into masochism, scopophilia into exhibitionism, love into hate, and vice versa.

"Instincts and their vicissitudes" discusses only the two more straightforward of the four vicissitudes Freud mentions: reversal into the opposite, and turning around on the subject. Even within those categories, the evident opposition between love and hate introduces complications, resulting in an extended discourse of surprising nuance.

INSTINCT DEFINED

The pleasure principle holds that our mind strives in general to lower the excitation impinging on it; pleasure, according to Freud's early writings, results from the lowering, and pain from the increase, of excitation. It follows that the first impetus to mental activity is the excitation that puts the pleasure principle into operation. Excitation can come in two varieties, stimuli impinging on the individual from the outside and those arising from within the individual. Freud called the latter variety "instinct" (*Trieb* in the original German).[1]

Freud considers *instinct* a provisional concept, an idea indispensible to articulating the workings of the mind yet whose precise definition was continually evolving. In a usage he recognizes as idiosyncratic, "instinct" refers to the mind's registration of stimuli flowing from an organ of the body resulting in a demand for "work" aimed toward the relief of the demand. Hunger and thirst are examples, as is the full panoply of sexual impulsions, including the stirrings of attraction, an infant's lust for thumb-sucking and physical contact, and

---

[1]   Although some contemporary authors writing in English cite "drives" rather than "instincts" for Freud's *Trieb*, I use "instincts," except when discussing those authors (see Epilogue), in accordance with the English translation in the *Standard Edition of the Complete Psychological Works of Sigmund Freud* (J. Strachey, Ed. and Trans.). See Note 81 of the Epilogue here.

the canonical sexual act. These promptings from our interior impinge on the mind, as do those emanating from the external world detected by the senses, including sights, sounds, smells, and things touched; the latter, however, do not produce the demand for work produced by the needs arising from interior stimuli.

Freud distinguishes four constituents of an instinct.

* The *force* or pressure of an instinct is its demand for work, or pressure toward activity. Hunger pangs inherently call for their removal.

* All instincts have an *aim*, and they have the same aim, namely satisfaction, which they achieve when they effect the elimination of the internal stimuli at their source. Many do, however, admit multiple pathways to their aim. For example, where sadistic impulses cannot safely discharge against their intended target, they may become redirected toward the self in the form of masochism: we want to lash out against a parent for restraining our impulses and assail ourselves instead.[2] Instincts can also become "inhibited" in their aim (Freud, 1915a, p. 122) and thus able to fulfill it only partially. Such is the fate of children's erotic impulses when children internalize their parents at the end of the Oedipal period; we internalize the love objects we could not possess erotically, thereby eliminating the erotic aim we had with respect to them (see Chapters 9–11 here).

* Instincts have an *object* through which they are able to achieve their aim. Our parents are the first objects of our erotic, or sexual, instincts, for instance. Objects become attached to instincts as a result of experience, in particular the experience of satisfaction. For example, parents become children's first love objects as a result of their gratification of children's needs, including their need for love. Instincts may change their objects. We gradually replace our parents with other people as objects of our erotic (sexual) urges.

The interchangeability of objects is instincts' most fluid characteristic. It, or its opposite in the form of fixation to a

---

2   See Chapter 11 for elaboration of that process of reversal of aggressive aim.

particular object, forms the basis of character development, symptom formation, and cultural development. In a case of fixation, a boy's continued erotic striving for his mother may result in the selection of later objects in her image (an "anaclitic" object choice: see Chapter 4). Or, in an illustration of character formation, we may take on the traits of a loved object when we must abandon our erotic strivings for the object. In the realm of symptom formation, aborted sexual development can produce a fetish, the replacement of a sexual object with our own body part.

* The *source* of an instinct is the organ or body part that generates the stimulus that reaches the mind in the form of the instinct, the stomach in a case of hunger for instance.

THE IMPACT OF INSTINCTS

In illustrating the particular potency of instincts in our mental life, Freud asks us to recall that an organism's first impulse is to discharge stimuli of any kind, given the primary function of the nervous system to relieve itself of excitation. This is the design of the reflex, the most primitive action of which the organism is capable (see Chapter 2 here). The reflex operates most readily on stimuli originating from outside the individual like a hot stove, from which we immediately withdraw our hand in a single action.

But neither this response nor any other kind of motor retreat works against internal, or instinctual, stimuli. We cannot withdraw from our stomach as we can from a hot stove. The only way to eliminate instinctual needs is to satisfy them.

Freud concludes it is the satisfaction of instinctual needs that impels the development of the mind, contrary to the conventional view that new input from the external world motivates change (Freud, 1915a, p. 120). As we saw earlier (see Chapter 2), individuals, to satisfy their basic needs, must renounce the primordial function of warding off stimuli, in favor of discerning the real circumstances and bringing about their alteration. Although hunger can be warded off in the immediate instance with hallucinated satiety, we must, to satisfy it in the long term, allow its pain, discern the absence of real nourishment, and set about obtaining the real thing. The task of fulfilling our instinctual needs, in Freud's vision, prompted the high level of development of the human nervous system.

Freud adds an important piece to this story in "Instincts and their vicissitudes." The imperviousness of instinctual needs, such as hunger, to mechanical withdrawal – as of a hand from a hot stove – forces a critical distinction on us, between stimuli we can escape and those we cannot. That distinction corresponds roughly to the difference between our interior and the external world, thus making way for the reality principle.

TYPES OF INSTINCTS

Although we could distinguish any number of instincts, a play instinct, a social instinct, and so on, Freud asks whether all such urges might not trace to a small number of irreducible ones. He identifies two, the sexual and ego instincts, as of this writing.

Freud finds the main justification for this division in the conflicts he has repeatedly observed clinically between the interests of the two categories. Patients in treatment uncover long-buried lusts, and animosities, toward love-objects; at the same time they uncover dread of those feelings, which they perceive as inappropriate and at risk for producing dangerous repercussions. In Freud's taxonomy, the lusts and animosities, both components of how we relate to our love objects, express the sexual instinct, and the fear of repercussions is a manifestation of the ego, or self-preservative, instinct. That the two categories of instinct can conflict suggests they form discrete entities.

The division also echoes the conventional distinction between hunger and love, where hunger connotes the ego instincts and love connotes the sexual instincts. The separation also follows biologically. Biology distinguishes between those functions that serve the individual and those aimed toward preservation of the species. The ego instincts have as their object the sustenance of the individual, while the sexual instincts serve to perpetuate the species. Both classes of instincts function from birth, and each undergoes a lengthy and somewhat separate development (see Chapter 2), though they may initially converge in some of the same acts. Babies sucking at the breast for nutrition may also discover the stimulatory pleasure of sucking in itself.

Freud says conscious experience gives no direct evidence of our instinctual life. The clinical analysis of the psychoneuroses has afforded the clearest clues. However, the clues have given evidence primarily of the sexual instincts, whose disturbance Freud concluded precipitates neurosis; the ego instincts – of which hunger and the will to power are examples (Freud, 1917b, p. 137) – have eluded observation. Freud therefore uses the sexual instincts to expand on the operation of both groups of instincts, although he recognizes the tactic may produce an overemphasis on sexuality.

THE VICISSITUDES OF INSTINCTS

Instincts, it turns out, are volatile. They can act vicariously for one another and, as already noted, can change their objects easily. Freud calls these shifts *vicissitudes* of the instincts, by which he means alterations in what is materially the same impulse. When, for example, he describes masochism as a "vicissitude" of sadism, and vice versa, he is supposing the same urge – the wish to dominate and ultimately to injure – has become redirected. Our urge to crush our mother has regrouped into a flagellation of self; the self-flagellation, when it arises as a vicissitude, is not a new, independent impulse.

Freud says vicissitudes arise throughout life either as part of a natural development whereby one activity evokes and gives way to another or as a defense when an instinctual impulse meets with an obstruction. Regarding the latter possibility, our animosity toward our mother might raise the terrifying specter of the loss of mother's love and protection. We may more safely beat up on ourselves.

Freud determines that an instinct may undergo any of four vicissitudes: reversal into the opposite instinct, turning around on the self, repression of the instinct, and sublimation of it. "Instincts and their vicissitudes" treats only the first two, reversal into the opposite and turning around on the self. Freud discusses repression in a separate paper (see Chapter 6). Although he touches on sublimation in numerous writings, the targeted treatment of sublimation to which he alludes here may have appeared in a lost paper.[3]

The first two processes – the ones Freud treats here – are simple direct transformations of an impulse into another impulse.

In *reversing into its opposite*, Freud says, an instinct can undergo either of two sub-processes. Its aim can change from active to passive while the content of the instinct remains the same. This occurs when, for example, instead of looking at others' body parts (scopophilia), people instead display themselves so as to be looked at. The second way in which an instinct can reverse into its opposite is that its content can reverse, as happens when our love of another – apparently, as Freud will clarify – changes to hate.

The vicissitude of *turning around on the self* overlaps with the active–passive version of reversing into the opposite, though only in the direction of active to passive, and only in part. For example, we may turn the rage we want to vent at a loved one on ourselves, thus deflecting a sadistic urge toward a masochistic one. But if the transformation stops there, with a wish for our own suffering, then it realizes only a turning of the instinct around on the self and not a complete reversal of our role from active to passive. We want only to be battered, by ourselves or anyone else; we do not want to suffer at the hands of a given other.

Two primitive sexual instincts exemplify the first of the two manifestations of the vicissitude of reversal into the opposite, namely the change from an active to a passive aim; in the process of doing so, they also display the turning around of an instinct on the self. They are

---

3   See the Editor's Note (James Strachey) to Freud's Metapsychological papers, *SE, XIV*, pp. 105–106. *1957*

the pairs sadism and masochism, and scopophilia and exhibitionism. In shifting from gazing upon another (scopophilia) to exposing ourselves so as to be looked at (exhibitionism), we both reverse the aim of the impulse from active to passive – from looking at an object to being looked at by someone else – and turn the impulse – to look – around on the self: the looking is now directed at us instead of away from us. The only instance of the reversal of content, the second manifestation of the reversal into the opposite of which Freud is aware, is the (apparent) change of love into hate. That apparent transformation, along with others in which love participates, introduces additional complexities.

In the light of the overlap between the active–passive reversal of an instinct and the turning around of an instinct on the self, and the independence of those two trends from the reversal of content, the ensuing reconstruction follows Freud in elaborating the vicissitudes in that order.

The reversal into the opposite and turning an instinct around on the self: the cases of sadism–masochism and scopophilia–exhibitionism

As Freud notes in his *Five Lectures...* (see Chapter 1 here) the two instinct pairs sadism–masochism and scopophilia–exhibitionism stand out among children's earliest, otherwise-autoerotic sexual activities in the engagement of an external object. In them we attempt to inflict cruelty on, or to be assailed by, another (sadism–masochism); or we try to look at the body of, or to be looked at by, another (scopophilia–exhibitionism).

Sadism and masochism

When he wrote "Instincts and their vicissitudes" Freud believed sadism precedes and provides the basis for masochism. It begins in early childhood when sadism involves acting for dominance over the family pet, for example. Small children who torture a pet do not intend to inflict pain, the canonical aim of developed sadism; rather, they are acting to control the animal and are unaware of any consequence for the animal. Only once they experience the result of the same act themselves, and connect the two – they know what it feels like to have a body part tugged on, for example – the production of the experience in another can become the aim of the violence they exercise. The pathway there might unfold as follows.

At this early phase in the development of the instinct, when we pull the cat's tail only to dominate and control the pet, it might come to pass that a loved authority forbids the act. After that we divert the impulse toward battery onto ourselves for safety – or even in anger toward the authority, an anger we dare not vent directly. Alternatively, the idea of pulling on our own body part might arise spontaneously by association with the pleasure of pulling on the body part of another. Either way, we now experience the pain the act can bring. The experience of pain verges on sexual excitation and hence brings a measure of pleasure, as Freud has noted (see Chapter 4) and will elaborate more fully later (see Chapter 10). We may now, therefore, seek to reproduce the pleasure. The repetition of the act for the purpose is masochism, though not yet in the form Freud considered fully developed.

Once the experience of pain becomes our objective, the sadistic aim of causing pain in another can arise, Freud infers. The instinct reverses once again, this time back toward the object, whose pain becomes masochistically enjoyed by the subject through his or her identification with the object.

A further development may occur in masochism itself, beyond the wish to achieve the stimulation created by pain. People come to wish to suffer at the hands of a specific other, who now in consequence takes over the role of subject or agent of the action. They like the idea of affiliating this other with the stimulation they achieve, or perhaps with the pain; abusive relationships might generate the latter as an aim. As of this writing Freud believed true masochism arises in only this more evolved and passive form, namely the desire to suffer at the hand of a real or imagined other; later (see Chapters 10 and 11) he recognizes a more primitive form of masochism independent of any wish to suffer at another's hand.

In passing, he distinguishes the feeling of pity as another possible opposite to sadism, an opposite in content, and hence as a candidate for another vicissitude of sadism. Pity connotes suffering with another, or feeling compassion for him or her. However, Freud says, pity is not a direct transformation of the instinct embodied by sadism and thus is not a vicissitude of it. At most it may arise as a reaction-formation against a sadistic impulse. It arises in that case as a separate impulse to cover the sadistic one (Freud, 1915a, p. 126).

Scopophilia and exhibitionism

A progression similar to that exhibited by sadism and masochism arises in the development of the instincts to look at another's organs (scopophilia) and to exhibit oneself (exhibitionism) and can be summarized briefly. First we are captivated by another's body and look at it. Next we give up the object and direct the impulse toward our own body, on account of dynamics similar to those that operate in the reversals between sadism and masochism. Lastly we introduce a subject to whom we want to display ourselves so as to be looked at by that person, who as a result of doing the looking becomes the agent, or subject, of the action.

Freud supposes that, in the case of scopophilia–exhibitionism, a primitive stage exists bearing no equivalent in the case of sadism–masochism, in which our attention becomes piqued by a part of our own body. This piece of autoeroticism carries the mark of the two opposite trends, the active and passive versions of looking-at (scopophilia and exhibitionism, respectively), that will emerge from it. On the one hand, the subject wants (actively) to look – at an organ. On the other hand, the subject, or the subject's organ, is (passively) being looked at.

Freud emphasizes, regarding both pairs, sadism–masochism and scopophilia–exhibitionism, that when individual instincts undergo the vicissitudes he has enumerated, something of their original form remains; thus different vicissitudes of the instinct come to exist side by side. As a result, Freud suggests, we may describe the instincts as "ambivalent" in their aims (Freud, 1915a, p. 131). We want to beat (someone) *and* be beaten, or, we want to look at (someone) *and* be looked at.

Freud sees in the reversal of the instinct's aim specifically into a passive one, in which the self becomes the object rather than the subject of the action, also a possible primitive avenue of defense against the active form of the instinct. For whereas the active instincts, to torture or gaze at another, bring the threat of reprisal, reversing the instincts into their passive form allows us to evade the threat. The more evolved vicissitudes of repression or sublimation are built around that purpose of defense, when acting on impulses might raise the threat of reprisal.

In the reversal into the opposite, the reversal of content: love and hate

The reversal of the content, as opposed to of the direction, of an instinct into its opposite takes place only in the apparent transformation of love into hate, Freud believes. In that metamorphosis, love and hate present the most striking example of ambivalent impulses. However, love and hate exist on a different plane from that of the pairs sadism–masochism and scopophilia–exhibitionism. Whereas the latter pairs, which involve specific behaviors, form only single components of the sexual trend, love and hate pertain to the whole current of it.

Moreover, love and hate are not simple polar opposites as sadism–masochism and scopophilia–exhibitionism are. They emerge from different sources, becoming opposites only during development. Loving, Freud says, participates in three oppositions, rather than only one. In addition to opposing hating, loving occupies the pole opposite being loved. And, loving and hating together form the opposite of indifference. Still, the interplay of love and hate holds the greatest significance and interest of the three pairs, and Freud dwells mainly on it.

The pair loving and being loved follows the same pattern of reversing active and passive aims as the pairs sadism–masochism and scopophilia–exhibitionism do. Like scopophilia–exhibitionism it also admits of a primitive phase that combines the active and passive attitudes. That phase, in the case of loving and being loved, is represented by narcissism, or loving oneself. When we love ourselves, we are both the object of our love and the subject who loves.

The condition of narcissism also undergirds the oppositions between love and hate and love–hate and indifference. The latter polarity, as the more primordial of the two, emerges when the early narcissistic ego, in achieving its sexual satisfactions autoerotically, has no need of the external world in achieving those satisfactions. The external world is thus indifferent, and a primitive version of the opposition love–indifference obtains.

The genesis of love and hate

Hating has its forerunner in the relation of the ego, or what will become the ego, to stimuli. The first function of the nervous system is to discharge stimuli, so as to reach a state of quiescence (see Chapter 2). Therefore, initially, the external world, with its afflux of stimuli, is hated, in the sense of presenting as something to be gotten rid of. But individuals at this stage do not distinguish internal and external worlds, let alone self and object. They know only pain and pleasure, either of which can come from – what the observer knows to be – within or without.

Hate-proper begins when objects intrude into the narcissistic universe. This they will necessarily do when the self-preservative instincts introduce external objects, for instance the breast, to the ego. For by contrast with the sexual instincts, which have no need of the external world to achieve satisfaction, the self-preservative instincts must engage that world to attain fulfillment. And when in fact the narcissistic ego satisfies its self-preservative instincts, for example eliminating hunger by taking nourishment, it finds the experience pleasurable, despite the inclusion of the external world.

When, in this context, an object becomes perceived as a source of pleasure, we love it, which is to say, according to Freud, we want to lessen the space between ourselves and the object; in the language of the most primitive manifestation of love we want to incorporate it into ourselves, as in take into the mouth (see also Freud, 1925a; Chapter 6, here, under "A conscious circumventing of repression").[4] Conversely, when an object becomes a source of displeasure, we hate it and want to distance ourselves from it. Indifference, once the forerunner of hate and the ultimate mark of distancing ourselves from something, now regroups after these developments, Freud adds, as a special case of hate.

Defining his terms more precisely, Freud (1915a, pp. 136–137) says that when an object becomes a source of pleasurable feelings, we set up a motor urge (p. 137) to bring it closer to the ego and incorporate it; we call this an attraction exercised by the object, and we say we love it. But when the object provokes unpleasurable feelings, we seek to increase the distance between it and the ego, mirroring our original attempts to flee the bombardment of stimuli from the external world; we say of the object in that case that it repels us and that we hate it.

Disjunctions between love and hate

The account of love and hate thus far depicts the two impulses as emerging from different, though paradigmatically opposite, sources. Love arises from an incorporative urge and hate from an impetus toward repulsion, or flight. Freud notes additional asymmetries between the two.

[4]   Freud (1915a) derives as a consequence of the tendency toward incorporation, or *introjection* (after Ferenczi, 1909), that the boundary between the ego (inner world) and the external world now shifts. Previously, we distinguished the inner and outer worlds on the basis of stimuli we could and could not escape from, inescapable stimuli consisting of instinctual needs and hence representing the internal world (see earlier this chapter under "The impact of instincts"). Freud calls the ego so defined the original "reality-ego" (1915a, p. 136). But now, given to taking into ourselves all we find pleasurable, and "projecting" all that is painful even if internal (Freud, 1913b; Chapter 3 here) we lose that "objective" (Freud, 1915a, p. 136) boundary. Instead we recognize as the line between the ego and external world that between what we find pleasurable and what we find either unpleasant or indifferent. Thus develops a pure "pleasure-ego," or primary narcissism.

He says that although we can experience love toward those objects that serve our sexual, or more broadly libidinal, instincts, we do not experience it toward objects that only serve our ego, which is to say our self-preservative needs. The latter objects enlist our dependency and perhaps a reduced form of love, such as fondness. Thus, love emerges as affiliated with the ego's pure pleasure-relations to its objects, attaching eventually to those that serve its sexual needs in the narrow sense.[5]

Hate, meanwhile, has no specific association with sexual pleasure or the sexual function. It attaches to unpleasure in general. The ego hates any object it perceives to cause it unpleasure. And it does not matter whether the unpleasure arises in the realm of sexual satisfaction or in the individual's pursuit of the instincts of self-preservation. Freud speculates that hate may derive more from the ego's struggle to survive and maintain itself than from sexual life; that struggle begins in the ego's attempt to distance itself from stimuli. In the light of that origin, hate remains closely associated with the self-preservative instincts.

These asymmetries reinforce the view that love and hate arise from separate sources, despite our perception of them as simple opposites. Freud surmises they then develop independently of one another before becoming organized as opposites.

Ambivalence: the conjunction of love and hate
Despite their disparate origins, love and hate overlap in their early development, and it is that overlap that prepares the way for the ambivalence between love and hate so ubiquitous in human relationships. Before we achieve the synthesis of the sexual instincts under the genitals and the corresponding development of mature love,[6] love

---

5   Loving in this full-blown sense, Freud says, becomes possible only after the various component sexual instincts have become integrated, which they do under the primacy of the genitals and in the service potentially of reproduction. This sequence accords with the idea that loving applies only to the ego as a whole and not to individual instincts.

6   See Note 5, preceding.

becomes focused in activities in which it overlaps with hate, rather than opposing it.

The first such focus is the oral zone, the original area to become a seat of sexual stimulation (see Chapter 1). Love in connection with that focus centers around the aim of incorporating or devouring the object (Freud, 1915a, p. 138). To incorporate or devour the object is to eliminate it as an entity – an outcome aligned with hate – as well as to embrace, or love, it. Thus, at this stage love and hate, or their fore-runners, are fused.

They remain that way in the next focus to emerge, the anal–sadistic organization. Love here manifests as an urge for mastery over the object; in the context of that aim, the individual is not concerned with whether the object becomes injured or annihilated. The urge for mastery naturally affiliates with self-preservation and therefore implies the involvement of the self-preservative/ego instincts. Thus, Freud thinks, the anal–sadistic sexual organization not only partakes of, but is dominated by, the ego instincts. As a result of that connec-tion it makes sense that the anal–sadistic organization would exude the impression of hate, because hate expresses the self-preservative instincts.

The changing relations between love and hate, which as we have seen become opposites once the sexual organization reaches full inte-gration (see Note 4, this chapter), explain the frequent occurrence of ambivalence in love. Partly, Freud says, remnants of the early stages in which love and hate merge remain. A contribution also comes from the ego instincts, which, in view of their frequent conflicts with love, find grounds for repudiation of the object in contemporary motives; for example, wary of possible rejection, we may feel distaste for the object we also love.

In a special case of intermixed love and hate, when parties to a love-relationship end that relationship, hate often replaces the love that has vanished. The sequence suggests love has transformed into hate, as though, indeed, the two were direct vicissitudes of one another. However, in addition to the self-evident objection that the hate may have its own contemporary motives, a different process may be at work. The severing of the love-relation sends the love impulses into regression, as they look for an opportunity for discharge. When love reaches the sadistic stage, it becomes deformed and takes on a cruel and hostile coloring, whereupon it easily fuses with the hate the individual already feels. In this fusion the regressed love lends an erotic character to the individual's hate and thus assures the continuity of the love-relation.

6 The possibility of repression: "Repression" (1915b); "Negation" (1925a)

> It is not easy in theory to deduce the possibility of such a thing as repression.
>
> – S. Freud, "Repression," 1915b, p. 146

Our impulses are fated to meet with obstruction, none more arresting than the threat of negative repercussions should we act on an impulse that produces them. Repression, like the "vicissitudes" in which impulses reverse into their opposite or turn around on the self (see Chapter 5), *affords a way in which we may avoid such repercussions. It is a complicated way, involving an action by the entire ego fearful not only of bad material consequences, but also of a fall in its worth; sublimation has the same origin but employs a different mechanism of deflection. Of all the vicissitudes an instinct may undergo, repression inflicts the greatest psychological cost.*

Repression consists of barring entry of a germinating impulse into consciousness in order to keep it from discharging. It operates by prompting a withdrawal of consciousness from the impulse, much as we might withdraw our hand from a hot stove. But because it flows from a judgment, however fleeting and unthinking, Freud characterizes it as falling between flight, which the withdrawal from a hot stove would represent, and condemnation, an act of deliberative judgment (1915b, p. 146).

This chapter tracks Freud's principal paper on repression (1915b), *addressing, in turn, the conceptual puzzle raised by repression, the course of repression, and its psychological cost. The paper seeds Freud's later paper on negation, which provocatively illustrates a conscious equivalent of repression and offers an illuminating reconceptualization of the pleasure and reality principles. The chapter concludes with a brief discussion of that paper.*

"REPRESSION" (1915b)

Instinctual impulses inherently seek discharge. Discharging them produces pleasure; not discharging them creates pain. But, Freud points out, although satisfying an impulse always leads to pleasure, satisfaction of, say, an incestuous or hostile urge could also cause *un*pleasure on account of other interests; those other interests might include safety, our parents' love and protection, or others' approbation. When the motive to avoid the unpleasure associated with satisfaction of an impulse becomes stronger than the motive to attain the pleasure expected from it we may *repress* the impulse.

Although the same considerations also drive the simpler vicissitudes (see Chapter 5), repression engages additional ones. We feel we as a person are bad for harboring the impulse in question. As Freud says in his earlier paper on narcissism (see Chapter 4): "Repression . . . proceeds from the ego; we might say with greater precision that it proceeds from the self-respect of the ego" (1914, p. 93). It responds to an appraisal of self above and beyond the fear of outside consequences.[1]

Phases of repression

Freud sees evidence of two phases of repression. Initially, in what he calls *primal repression*, we withdraw consciousness from the offending impulse, which, because it has not discharged, continues to exist unconsciously, unaltered. Thus, Freud's patient Elisabeth von R. lost awareness of the fleeting – and heinous, in her view – thought she had by the deathbed of her beloved sister that her brother-in-law, to whom she had felt an unacknowledged attraction, would now be free to marry

---

[1] In this early writing, Freud concerns himself with the repression specifically of our impulses – on whose account we might perceive the self as worthy or unworthy. In his later *Outline of Psychoanalysis* (1940a) he ascribes repression a broader compass, including our memory of external events, for example actions witnessed by or done to us, and not only actions we committed or contemplated.

her (see Chapter 1). A second stage follows, *repression proper*, in which lines of thought initially unconnected with the repressed impulse become associatively linked with it and as a result become repressed, as well; Freud calls that result *after-pressure* (Freud, 1915b, p. 148).

The increasing reach of the repression – the repression proper – derives from two simultaneously operating processes, Freud says. One is the primal repression, the ejection of the initial impulse from consciousness and hence Elisabeth von R.'s banishment from consciousness of her lustful thought about marrying her brother-in-law. With respect to the other process, the impulses that have become repressed draw to them, and hence into repression, any additional content with which they can establish even a remote connection. Thus, once Elisabeth von R. had repressed impulses attesting to her attraction to her brother-in-law, other memories suggestive of the circumstance – other moments of passion aroused by the brother-in-law or more distally related familial events – slipped into repression as well (Breuer and Freud, 1893–1895, pp. 135–181).

Repression and the psychoneuroses

Freud notes as a critical characteristic of repression that it must remain in constant operation to hold the forbidden impulse – always pressing for expression – at bay, lest it break through. On account of the persistence of the conflict that prompted the repression and remains unresolved, repression provides the basis for the psychoneuroses.

Additionally, the lack of conscious monitoring of repressed impulses allows them to grow in both strength and associative reach. Some associations form to contents far enough removed from the original impulse that they are able to find conscious expression via those contents. At the same time the association of the expressed contents with the original impulse, separated by countless haphazard interstitial steps, eludes consciousness. Absent its detection of the original impulse, consciousness cannot sense the danger that provoked its repression of the impulse. It thus allows some remotely associated expressions to manifest as symptoms; they manifest compulsively, as typifies symptoms, because they are driven by the unconscious and hence unknown and unresolved impulse at their base.

The occurrence of these associations and their eventual manifestation in symptoms makes possible the treatment of neurotics by psychoanalysis. The process of free association, the signature tool of psychoanalysis, begins with those thoughts patients are able to express and proceeds through the chain of associations they generate thereafter until they can go no further. At that point, psychoanalytic experience shows, patients have come close to uncovering the originally forbidden content. In feeling they can progress no further in their associations, they are actually repeating their original attempt at repression of the offending impulse – but now the attempt at repression has been brought into the open, so patient and therapist can track it and work it through.

Repressed impulses, although fully preserved and able to proliferate, do not remain intact once repressed. The idea and the affect, or emotion, associated with the repressed impulse receive different treatment, and that difference is what makes way for symptoms. The idea – in Elisabeth von R.'s case the thought that she might marry her brother-in-law – is kept from consciousness. The affect – Elisabeth von R.'s passion and her horror at it – meets one of three fates: it is suppressed altogether; it is realized as an affect though detached from the idea to which it was originally connected – Elisabeth von R..s leg pains; or it is transformed specifically into anxiety. Should the energy indeed manifest in anxiety or another unpleasant form, such as debilitating pain, then the repression has failed: the purpose of repression is to avoid unpleasure (Freud, 1915b, pp. 152–153).

Freud, having observed that repression lies at the root of the psychoneuroses, infers it often leaves *substitute formations* in its train. Those are distortions of repressed impulses that, like Elisabeth von R.'s leg pains, have found expression on account of their ample remoteness from the repressed impulse – in her case, her affection for her brother-in-law and the idea that she might marry him. In addition to pathological formations like symptoms, they include parapraxes – minor lapses of everyday thought and speech like slips of the tongue (see Chapter 1) – and jokes.

Freud determines that these formations must result not from repression itself but from a separate process, because they directly oppose the aim of repression, which is to eliminate the unwanted impulse. In arising as substitutes for the repressed impulse, they allow partial satisfaction of it. Symptoms and other substitute formations, Freud says, indicate a *return of the repressed* (Freud, 1915b, p. 154), meaning that the forbidden impulses, made to disappear via the repression, have resurfaced, although in altered form. In a case of pathology they can signal an early step toward returning health, given that the repression has been breached, although the success is only partial and difficult to detect. Anna O.'s inability to drink illustrates this dynamic: her paralysis partly articulates the content of the original scene – the idea of drinking – and expresses the withheld affect – of disgust, here transformed into an inability to take any nourishment by drinking (see Chapter 1).

Repression and psychoneuroses: examples of symptom-formation

Repression, as the mind's reflexive attempt to avoid unpleasure, results in a withdrawal of energy from impulses anticipated to provoke danger. In a final demonstration of the potent and complex sequelae it can generate, Freud offers examples of repression and symptom formation in the three different psychoneuroses best known to him.

Anxiety hysteria

He first addresses *anxiety hysteria*, as it manifests in animal phobias, which, Freud surmises, replace dread of the father. He proposes more specifically based on clinical case analyses that patients repress a lust for a parent, typically the father, combined with a fear of him. As a consequence of that repressing, the father vanishes from the patient's conscious libidinal life; he is replaced by an animal to which the patient has had the occasion to respond with anxiety – it is terrifying or threatening in some way – and which is connected with the father along a chain of associations. The subject of Freud's "Little Hans" case history (1909b), for example, had, between three and five years of age, developed a fear of big animals, especially horses, because they had big "widdlers" (penises); he had become fascinated with penises, including his father's. The father, so represented, forms the content of the repressed impulse, while the affective portion of the impulse, consisting of the lust for, combined with the fear of, him transforms into anxiety. The process results in a replacement of the lust for the father with the fear of the animal.

A repression of this kind fails in its aim to remove the unpleasure associated with the repressed impulse, because, even though the original ideational target – the father – is exchanged for a substitute, the substitute itself is a scary one, so it produces marked anxiety instead of pleasure. That result pushes the process to a second and main phase of the disease, in which the phobia forms; thereafter, dread of the animal dominates and compulsive measures, like avoidance of any area where the animal is likely to pass, are designed to prevent the outbreak of anxiety.

Conversion hysteria

A different configuration of processes operates in the second class of neuroses Freud discusses, *conversion hysteria*, alternately shortened to *hysteria*. Hysteria has as a distinguishing feature the disappearance of the affect connected with the repressed complex, such as the fear that dominated Little Hans. In its place hysterics display indifference, as, for example, when a sufferer who has developed a tic consisting of an intrusive clacking sound shows no worry about the disorder.

The ideational portion of the impulse in conversion hysterias vanishes completely, as it does in phobias (anxiety hysterias). Typically an excessive somatic innervation of another function, usually a sensory or motor one, appears in its place. The innervation may manifest either as an excitation, as in the case of an uncontrollable tic, or an inhibition, as in the case of a paralysis like Anna O.'s inability to drink. The over-agitated area turns out on closer inspection to form part of the repressed impulse; Anna O.'s inhibition in drinking, having originated in her (unexpressed) disgust at the governess' dog's drinking from a cup, is again an example. Freud says the agitated area has taken over the full share of psychical energy animating the repressed impulse, thereby *condensing* it into a narrow and distorting focus (Freud, 1915b, p. 156).

Obsessional neurosis

Obsessional neurosis, the third disorder Freud discusses as a window on repression, presents yet another dynamic. An obsessional neurotic represses a hostile impulse that already represents a substitution for a tender one; for instance, an afflicted person's animosity toward his father replaces erotic strivings toward him.[2] The harboring of hostile impulses against someone the individual loves triggers the repression, which succeeds in holding the unsupportable feeling at bay at first. In this one stroke, both the content and the affect of the unwanted impulse disappear; the person does not know he harbors hostility against his father, and he does not feel hostile toward him or a substitute.

In place of the banished idea and affect, by means of what Freud terms a *reaction-formation*, an increased sensitivity of conscience appears, in which the person stays on the alert for his slightest moral failure. In a reaction-formation people experience an exaggerated version of the impulse opposite the one they have repressed; thus, extreme sensitivity to our moral failings replaces barbarous hostility, for instance.[3] Freud suspects the result is facilitated by the ambivalent

---

[2]   As a first step in defense, the substitution comes about by means of a developmental regression on the part of the tender impulse toward sadism, Freud says.

[3]   Interestingly, Freud does not believe this phase of the disease, in which exaggerated moral sensitivity replaces animosity via reaction-formation, represents a return of the repressed – a breaking through of the originally repressed impulse. What has happened

relation that underlies obsessional neurosis: the individual harbors both love and hate for the same object.

That ambivalence eventually wears down the repression and allows the repressed impulse slowly to return, however. The vanished affect – the hostility – reappears as now-intense moral anxiety laced with endless self-reproaches, and the content of the impulse – the idea that we loathe a particular love object – moves to a new scene of action. The new scene of action often involves something small and insignificant. In that new venue the illness trends toward a full recreation of the repressed complex. The opposition between equally powerful love and hate results in a paralysis of the will (Freud, 1909c, p. 241), in which people become incapable of reaching a decision about any action that ought to be guided by love. The indecision extends to an increasingly wide field of behavior. The expansion follows, Freud says, from the lover's unconscious tendency to bring all pursuits within the compass of the drama playing out in this one completely absorbing facet of life.

The young lieutenant of Freud's (1909c) Rat Man case history acted out the ambivalence at the root of such behavior when he once compulsively moved a stone from the road his lady's carriage was to traverse. He didn't want the carriage to falter and harm its rider. But he then compulsively replaced the stone so the lady might indeed suffer (1909c, p. 192).[4] With the ideational content of the original impulse obstinately barred from consciousness, the struggle between the warring impulses carries on unceasingly.

Compulsions develop to compensate for the doubt and the excruciating inhibition the doubt inflicts. To the extent the patient manages to follow through with a decision, then it must be carried

instead, he says, is that the energy that animated the dangerous and consequently repressed impulse has shifted to the pole opposite the impulse – hence heightened conscience in place of the wish to destroy, thereby intensifying that pole. The mechanism therefore continues the action of repression, which consists in a withdrawal of energy from a threatening impulse.

4   Those who doubt their own love, Freud notes quoting Hamlet (Act II, Scene 2; cited in Freud 1915b, p. 241, Note 2), must doubt every lesser thing.

out. The decision at least allows discharge of the monumentally built-up energy resulting from the inhibition of the original impulse and the conflict to which it leads. The energy makes itself felt variously in commands and prohibitions, depending on whether an affectionate or hostile impulse gains access to discharge. If the patient cannot obey the command that has arisen, tension rises to an unbearable degree and is experienced as severe anxiety. The compensatory measures devolve from acts to the thoughts leading up to the acts. The thoughts then arise in the mind compulsively. Obsessive thinking results.

A CONSCIOUS CIRCUMVENTING OF REPRESSION: "NEGATION" (1925a)

Of all the mind's foibles, repression poses the greatest challenge to the treatment of psychoneuroses. Material buried within the mind precipitates the formation of a pathological entity that has compromised patients' lives. Absent the painstaking and prolonged intervention of an analysis, people cannot either access or excise the material.

Some clues emerge to aid the analytic process, among them dreams, symptoms, and the "transference" of earlier relationships onto the analyst. Each of these clues opens a channel into the repressed complex and thus provides a productive starting point for free association. But a potentially more direct path to significant material surfaces when patients spontaneously deny ideas they bring forth in the course of their analyses. The bringing forth followed by denial, or *negation*, of the idea affords the patient a way to bring the content to awareness without accepting it, as yet. For example, after a patient says she hadn't wanted any harm to come to her mother the day they stood together looking down a deep ravine, she considers the opposite prospect and slowly awakens memories of fleeting hostility she had felt toward her mother in the past.[5] Such negation, reflexive

---

[5]   Freud found he did not necessarily need to wait for a patient to generate a spontaneous denial of this kind. He could instead ask the patient what the least likely interpretation was of a given dream image, for example, and elicit a true and otherwise inaccessible answer.

and unconscious like repression yet verging on conscious operation, can be seen as falling between repression and conscious condemnation.[6]

Freud devotes the rest of his short paper on negation to the wider psychological implications of that clinical discovery. The observation that the negation of an assertion can signify the repression of the assertion leads him to wonder whether the ordinary judgment of a proposition's falsity – e.g., "No, his birthday is not May 21st" – might not have originated as a way of freeing, though not accepting, repressed material. The matter of judgments of falsity raised, he next incorporates that capability into the progression from the pleasure to the reality principle, now conceived with respect to the types of judgments each primes us to make.

Our judgments fall principally into two kinds, Freud says: they affirm or deny whether something has a given quality – good or bad, or useful or harmful – and they affirm or deny whether an impression exists in reality. Early in our development we judge only quality. In terms of our earliest instinctual impulses, the oral ones, we either want to take the entity into ourselves or we want to keep it outside. Later, in keeping with the reality principle, we determine not only whether we will take something into the ego, but also whether it exists outside or only inside us. More specifically, we want to know whether we can find again in reality the thing we found there before – a beloved other, for example – so we can seize it when we want it.

The need for the latter distinction comes into being when we can bring before the mind again something we have perceived before, such as the state of satiety or the image of mother, without its necessarily being there. When it isn't there, we do not achieve the satisfaction we expected from it. Once we can make the second kind of

---

6   The series within which Freud here inserts negation includes one still more primitive step, evident in "Repression" (1915b). Flight, from the painful or the frightening, arises as the first means by which we escape or deny something. Initially reflexive, flight is neither conscious nor deliberative. Repression follows, as the mental equivalent of flight, followed by negation and conscious condemnation, representing increasing consciousness and deliberation.

judgment, we can bring the object before the mind again knowing the difference between that image and the real one. We next either engage the object for its expected satisfactions if it is real or set about attaining it if it is not real (Freud, 1925a, pp. 238–239). That judgment thus determines our choice of action – engaging what is real in the expected way or mobilizing to attain it – and ends the postponement of action due to thought.[7]

Freud, extrapolating from these considerations, ventures that judgment represents an expedient continuation of the function of introjecting things into, and repulsing them from, ourselves according to the pleasure principle. It becomes possible when the creation of the symbol of negation, in freeing thought from the effects of repression, liberates it from the pleasure principle. Repression expresses sheer pleasure principle in its reflexive banishing of distressing content. Negation, however, although it too deflects pain, also allows some of it through and hence breaches the imperative of the pleasure principle.

---

[7]   Thought, in this elementary context, is an experimental action, a motor palpating as Freud now describes it, of possibilities for material action (Freud, 1925a, pp. 238–239).

7   The unconscious and the structure of the mind: "The unconscious" (1915c)

> Consciousness makes each of us aware only of his own states of mind;
> that other people, too, possess a consciousness is an inference which we
> draw by analogy from their observable utterances and actions . . . .
> Psychoanalysis demands nothing more than that we should apply this
> process of inference to ourselves also.
>
> – S. Freud, "The unconscious," 1915c, p. 169

*The action of repression creates a repository of thoughts and impulses
of which we remain unaware but that nonetheless influence our
conscious thought and behavior. The delineation of that repository
forms Freud's signature contribution to psychology, the designation
of an unconscious portion of the mind.*[1]

*In "The unconscious" (1915c), his landmark paper on the subject,
Freud justifies the existence of the unconscious, maps out its characteristics, and situates it in our broader mental ecology. He proposes a
mental "topography" that includes unconscious, preconscious, and
conscious processes, importantly clarifying that consciousness is tanta-
mount to a sensory organ that detects thought, which is itself unconscious. Within this frame he draws an intriguing comparison between
thought and emotion, deepens his analysis of the dynamics of repression, compares the characteristics of conscious and unconscious mentation, and addresses the communication between the two systems.*

*Psychoanalysis after Freud depends on this paper in spirit if not
in detail given that the existence of the unconscious in mental life is
foundational to all schools. Fields well beyond psychoanalysis, as
well as intellectual and popular culture, accept the major divisions*

---

[1] Freud conceived the unconscious as containing a small group of inherited impulses and
ideas, along with the preponderant repressed impulses, which derive from individual
experience (see Chapter 9, under "Ego and superego" for elaboration).

laid out here. The relation between thought and emotion remains an
active topic in modern psychological and philosophical discourse.

JUSTIFICATION FOR THE UNCONSCIOUS

Freud marshals several lines of evidence to document the existence of
unconscious mentation. These include dreams, psychoneurotic symptoms, and the small mental errors of daily life, like slips of the tongue, he
calls parapraxes. They also encompass the normal popping up of
thoughts whose source we cannot identify, the capacity of hypnosis to
reveal memories to which people have no conscious access, and our very
susceptibility to hypnotic suggestion. Psychoanalysis shows individual
happenings of these kinds to have had motives unavailable to consciousness at the time the happenings occurred. Indeed, Freud maintains,
conscious processes account for only a small percentage of our mental
activity.

By way of conceptual justification of the idea of an unconscious,
Freud points out, as per the epigraph to this chapter, we have direct
knowledge of only our own consciousness and infer others' consciousness by analogy from their behavior to ours. The assumption of an
unconscious, he says, requires only that we apply this same process of
inference to ourselves.

Mental processes in themselves are unconscious, on Freud's
view, and become detected by consciousness. We turn consciousness
to one or another mental content in the same way we turn our sense
organs to one or another stimulus in the outside world. What we
perceive of the internal or external world need not reflect that world
accurately, however. Just as Kant alerted us to the subjectivity of our
perception of the external world, consciousness may distort the
unconscious processes it reflects, Freud says. He believes we may
correct our conscious view of our unconscious processes – the objects
of our internal perception – because he believes the latter, being
internal, are more knowable than are external objects (Freud, 1915c,
p. 171). We have tools like psychoanalysis with which to understand

them, when, for example, arrival at an insight relieves a symptom as it did for Anna O.

TWO KINDS OF NON-CONSCIOUS MENTATION

Freud distinguishes two different kinds of non-conscious mental function. One consists of processes of which we are unaware and to which we cannot will access. It is for that kind of mental process, which includes repressed impulses, that Freud reserves the term *unconscious*. The other kind, which Freud calls *preconscious*, encompasses those thoughts and impulses of which we are unaware at the moment but of which we could easily become conscious if we were to focus on them. Although we may not be thinking at the moment about what we had for breakfast, we could easily retrieve the information.

This differentiation between unconscious and preconscious states adds nuance to the picture of how a thought becomes conscious, when it does. Thoughts, as noted, begin as unconscious. They undergo testing, which Freud calls *censorship*, to determine whether they may become conscious without threatening our sense of safety. If the censor finds them inadmissible they remain unconscious and in a state of repression; if they pass testing, they become preconscious. A different and less stringent set of criteria determines whether those thoughts will pass from their preconscious state all the way to consciousness. Thus, the major barrier thoughts need to cross is that between unconsciousness and preconsciousness. Because it is at that boundary that the characteristics of thought change, Freud often combines preconscious with conscious thought under the general label of consciousness for expository purposes.[2]

---

[2] Freud wonders in what form a thought passes from a state of unconsciousness to preconsciousness and consciousness. He envisions two possibilities. In one, the thought continues in its original form unconsciously while a fresh version of it registers in preconscious/conscious thought: the wish to annihilate our father continues unaltered in the unconscious, for example. In the other, only the original manifestation of the thought exists, and it changes state: the wish to annihilate the father, formerly unconscious, now becomes conscious, and no record of it remains in our unconscious. Freud answers his query at the end of the paper; see the end of the chapter here.

Although Freud, materialist he is, assumes the mental topography he has outlined – of unconscious, preconscious, and conscious operations of the mind – has a basis in our neuroanatomy, he emphasizes that the topography does not correspond point for point with its biological base. While leaving open the possibility that future science could support a different view, Freud will continue to warn against biological reductionism in his later writings.[3] Thus, we must bear in mind that when he speaks of different agencies or regions of the mind, he is not referring to any kind of physical reality.

UNCONSCIOUS EMOTION

The template of a succession from unconsciousness to consciousness applies less easily to emotion than it does to thought, Freud finds. For, whereas he can give sense to the idea of conscious emotions, he sees the concept of unconscious emotions as less intelligible, and as less intelligible than the concept of unconscious thought.

An emotion, or *feeling*, Freud elaborates, is by definition something that is felt, and he couples feeling with sensation and sensation with consciousness. Thus, for example, to smell something foul or touch something sharp is to be in a particular state of awareness; we do not think of such a state as lodged in the unconscious recesses of our minds and working its way forward to conscious perception. If we do not at this moment detect the foul odor we encountered a few hours ago, we would not, even if we remembered the smell, say we are smelling it now, consciously or unconsciously. It originates at the senses, and once it leaves them, it is gone. Freud envisions a related scenario for emotion. We *feel* sadness, now, consciously, or we do not. We may remember having felt it in the past, but are not by dint of remembering feeling sad now, consciously or unconsciously.

Yet clinical psychoanalysis turns on the very notion that we harbor emotions of which we are not aware – unconscious anger, guilt, or lust, among others. Their press forces various psychic accommodations.

---

[3]   In the opening chapter of *Civilization and its Discontents* he goes so far as to reject physical–spatial language as a way even of describing the mental metaphorically.

The accommodations, known as *defenses*, include the repression of threatening impulses and their associated emotion. The emotion, when under repression, may separate from the ideational content of the impulse and attach to a different content through a process known as *displacement*; an example might be lust for the mother manifesting in a craving for someone or something else. Alternatively, the original emotion may become converted into a different one, which Freud calls a *transformation of affect*, in which case the lust for the mother might become antipathy toward her.

Exemplifying these mechanisms, phobias, on Freud's analysis, originate in an erotic desire for a parent that is repressed, and hence made unconscious, and twice converted: it becomes first free-floating anxiety and later a fear specifically of a substitute object, like a horse (see Chapter 6 here) – via displacement, or a replacement of content. Sometimes repressed affects, like hostility, are simply suppressed, rather than replaced. In the related defense mechanism of reaction formation, someone may defend against unconscious hostility toward a loved one by replacing it with the opposite behavior, sycophantism.

When, as a result of its repression an emotion can no longer be felt consciously, it exists only in potential. To exist as an emotion it needs to be felt consciously, and because of the repression, the conscious experience of it is only potential. Hence the emotion is only potential. Lust for the father, latent but repressed – an unlit fuse in the unconscious – strives for release it cannot achieve. It is in this limited sense that we may speak of unconscious emotions – as processes awaiting discharge – by contrast with conscious emotions, which realize the discharge.

Thoughts differ in kind, according to Freud. Ideas, which form the contents of our thoughts, are evocations, he says, of what are essentially memory traces. They exist passively in the mind and may be illuminated – brought to awareness – or not, whereas emotion entails the going off, or potential going-off, of something. Thus, we harbor unconscious thought, but only unconscious potential emotion, which, however, is no less powerful for that status.

THE MECHANICS OF REPRESSION

Repression, in rendering an impulse unconscious, operates on the boundary between the conscious and the unconscious. As we have understood it thus far, it involves the withdrawal of consciousness from an impulse. That account would suggest, for example, that when Elisabeth von R. repressed the objectionable passing thought that now that her sister was dead she could marry her widowed brother-in-law (see Chapter 1), she withdrew consciousness from the thought. In "The unconscious" (1915c) Freud elaborates repression to include a second process, a pushing away of noxious impulses, in addition to the withdrawal of consciousness from them.

He depicts the dynamic in terms of displacements of psychical energy, or *cathexis*, which refers to an infusion of such energy; energy, of which there is a finite amount, is displaced any time the mind does anything. Impulses, he elaborates, enter into the states variously of unconsciousness, preconsciousness, and consciousness when the mind deploys energies capable of imbuing them with those respective qualities. Thus, an impulse gets repressed, or becomes unconscious after having been conscious, when the energy associated with consciousness is withdrawn from it.

The ascription of repression to only that process – of a withdrawal of energy – turns out, on inspection, to encounter difficulties. Impulses, once unconscious, can remain active. For example, they can manifest, disguised, in dreams. To remain active in that manner, an impulse must have retained the cathexis that originally animated it, leaving the question of what was withdrawn. Freud says it was conscious, as opposed to unconscious, cathexis. Elisabeth von R.'s thought itself – the idea of marrying the brother-in-law – was originally unconscious. As unconscious, the thought was animated by unconscious cathexis. It became conscious, or nearly so, by having been further illuminated by conscious cathexis, or energy affiliated specifically with consciousness. It is the latter energy that was withdrawn when the idea underwent repression.

Now Freud perceives a further puzzle. Insofar as an impulse has retained any kind of cathexis in the unconscious, nothing is to stop it from attempting again to penetrate into consciousness. Were it to do that, the withdrawal of conscious cathexis from it would have to be repeated, endlessly; Elisabeth von R. would have been (consciously) entertaining, or nearly entertaining, her objectionable thought and then repressing it, many times over. However, repression appears on the contrary to be an enduring condition; Elisabeth von R. simply had no memory of the thought. Additionally, some impulses form in the unconscious and remain there without ever receiving conscious cathexis.[4] Not having received any conscious cathexis, they cannot lose it. Yet, intuition tells us, they exist in a state of repression.

It is here that Freud recognizes that for an impulse to remain out of consciousness, and an affect to remain undeveloped, a different force must maintain the repression. He designates the exertion against the impulse as *anticathexis*. Anticathexis is the means by which the preconscious guards itself against the intrusion of the unconscious impulse. He suggests that this is all that happens in the case of *primal repression* when an impulse is initially forced from consciousness. At this juncture, in other words, the mind is only beating back an impulse – Elisabeth von R.'s thought – as opposed to withdrawing energy from it. But when *repression proper*, or the "after-pressure" exerted by unconscious material on the newly repressed idea, takes hold, then, Freud supposes, conscious cathexis is withdrawn as well.[5]

In the wake of this elaboration of repression Freud codifies what are now three ways of looking at psychological phenomena within psychoanalysis. The *dynamic* point of view conceives them in terms of the conflict or other combination of psychological forces, tracing ultimately to our instincts (see Chapter 5). The *topographical* point of view understands the phenomena with reference to the subsystems

---

4   We know of this possibility from psychoanalytic treatment that eventually uncovers impulses that have operated unconsciously, for example in producing dreams or symptoms, for a long time before becoming exposed.

5   See Chapter 6 on the different stages of repression.

operating in the mind, consisting, as of this paper, of the unconscious, preconscious, and conscious, and later of the id, ego, and superego (see Chapter 9). Lastly, the *economic* point of view, rooted in the amount and nature of psychological energy expended, characterizes mental life with reference to changes in volumes of that energy. The three vantage points together make up a *metapsychology* that depicts the mind's operation in broadest terms.

DISTINGUISHING CHARACTERISTICS OF THE CONSCIOUS AND UNCONSCIOUS

The unconscious possesses many characteristics that distinguish it from the conscious, the full complement of which Freud labels *primary process thought*, the most primitive and uninhibited mentation humans carry out. He describes the characteristics as follows.

*Wishful impulses, seeking to discharge their psychic energy (cathexis), including buried lusts, animosities, and impressions of things we felt threatened to have witnessed, form its core.

*Contrary impulses exist side by side and do not influence one another. Someone might (unconsciously) want both to kill his father and to have erotic intimacy with him and would not register in any way the incompatibility of those goals. Impulses verge on impacting one another only insofar as they find joint expression in an intermediate aim or compromise, as can be seen, for instance, in nail-biting, which expresses incorporation or embrace, on the one hand, and the tearing or destruction of something, on the other. Formations of this kind often appear in dream imagery, as well as in symptoms and parapraxes, all of which divulge unconscious impulses.

*The unconscious contains no function of judgment and hence knows no negation, doubt, or degrees of certainty. A son, in his unconscious, wants to murder his father, and he wants intimacy with him; he does not want maybe to murder him or wonder whether it would be a good idea. Impulses lacking that nuance press toward discharge only to a greater or lesser degree; their comparative strength determines the likelihood they will present in dream imagery, foment symptoms, or surface in a momentary disruption of conscious function in a parapraxis.

*Unconscious processes, in pressing only toward discharge, observe only the pleasure principle. They disregard reality. It does not matter that the son would never actually murder his father.

*The unconscious, in its disregard of reality, does not register time and is not influenced by it. It does not matter that the father is already dead.

*The different contents of the unconscious become linked through two hallmarks of primary process thought, *displacement* and *condensation*. We may think of displacement informally as the substitution of one idea for another, as occurred when Little Hans replaced his dread of his father with a fear of horses. Formally, Freud says what is happening is the energy – cathexis – animating the original impulse detaches from that impulse and passes along to another initially less charged idea related to the first through an associative chain: Little Hans noted the large "widdlers" on both horses and his father. In the case of condensation several impulses find expression in a single, or at any rate smaller group of, ideas. In terms of energy flow, a single idea (etc.) appropriates the energy of several other ideas, along different chains of association: Anna O.'s incapacity to drink embodied her disgust at the governess' dog's drinking from a human cup, that disgust itself already an expression of her displeasure with the governess. Displacement and condensation are notorious instruments of defense and surface in symptoms, parapraxes, and dreams and are most vividly illustrated by the last.

Consciousness, occupied by *secondary process thought*, contrasts with unconsciousness on all of these points.[6]

---

[6] James Strachey, general editor of the *Standard Edition* of Freud's psychological works, mentions a possible lost paper of Freud's on consciousness of which items mentioned in what follows may be an outline (Editor's Note 1, Freud (1915c), p. 192).

*Impulses that reach consciousness carry a natural inhibition toward discharge. We may feel a fury rise that our father has interfered yet again in our affairs, but in the same breath we contain the outrage and merely *think* about it.

*Conscious thought is sensitive to contradiction, which prompts a search for resolution. We can find it severely disquieting to feel affection and animosity toward the same person.

*Judgment and negation figure prominently in conscious thought. We judge whether things are good or bad, right or wrong, true or false, or in possession of other qualities such as attractiveness, roundness, and size. We deny assertions and reject possibilities. We can be doubtful or uncertain.

*Conscious thought, except in fantasy and wishful thinking, observes the reality principle, though it may choose to disregard it and, for example, ignore pending danger or the fact that a plan of action relies on fantasy. It is protected by *censorship*, of threatening impulses, which acts as a gateway to it.

*Ideas are ordered in time. We sequence events by "before" and "after" and gradations therein. Freud speculates in his later "Note upon the 'Mystic Writing-Pad'" (1925c) that the idea of time may derive from the circumstance that impressions can vanish from consciousness, whereas unconscious impressions remain indefinitely. We experience something – are conscious of it – and then it fades into a preconscious memory while subsequent (conscious) experiences arise; the remembered one came "before," and the conscious one "after."

*Displacement and condensation do not occur in conscious thought. Energy can pass in small amounts from one idea to the next, while the main quota of it remains with the original idea. Thus, although one idea will never fully replace another – whereby the cathexis of the original one would pass entirely over to the new idea – a secondary idea may receive some animation or interest by dint of its association with the first idea. A woman passionate for a man picking blueberries may, in yielding to displacement, find herself enamored of picking them herself. Ideas are, however, linked, but by comparison and reasoning, and they can influence one another. Thus, in conscious thought, our love for our father may cause us to temper the anger we also feel toward him.

Freud credits his mentor Josef Breuer with an important extrapolation from the last contrast between conscious and unconscious energy flow: psychic energy exists in two states. One, dominating unconscious processes, is freely mobile, or *free*, and pressing toward discharge. Urges simply exist – we lust for our father. No reason or reasoning intervenes. The second state of psychic energy, which dominates conscious mentation, is *bound*. We think, judge, forecast, and plan, rather than merely experience urges. The latter activities entail the displacement of small, measured amounts of energy. Those activities, as instances of thought, consume less energy than does actual action, which they replaced historically, the reduction in energy expenditure requiring a "binding" of the excess (see Chapter 2 here).

Summarizing, we might say the conscious incorporates and acts on impulses and thus contains more than mere impulse. It includes discursive thought, observation, judgment, and decision. It attempts to root out contradiction and carries out different kinds of negation; it rejects, denies, and disagrees. It admits of degrees of certainty and succumbs to doubt. It proceeds by reasoning and comparison. It remains largely governed by the reality principle, mostly separating off fantasy and wishful thinking, and it recognizes time.

The unconscious differs from the conscious not only in that it exists outside awareness but also in that it consists only of wishful impulses. Those know no contradiction, negation, or doubt and connect with one another by passing their strength from one to the other or by pooling it, in other words by displacement and condensation, respectively. The unconscious, or primary process thought, is less evolved than the conscious, or secondary process thought.

Freud thus leaves us with the idea that a part of the human personality exists that only wants. It does not think, doubt, or adhere to the rules of logic, all of which are add-ons to our original state, now embodied by our unconscious, which knows nothing of them. In compromised states, such as those brought about by psychopathology, the add-ons and the original processes separate, thus exposing the distinction between them.

POINTS OF CONTACT BETWEEN THE CONSCIOUS AND UNCONSCIOUS

Despite the litany of differences between the conscious and unconscious and the barrier between them in the form of censorship, pathways of influence exist between the two systems under normal as well as pathological conditions.

The unconscious remains active throughout life in everyone and impacts conscious and preconscious function. Sometimes, Freud says, an unconscious impulse aligns with a conscious one and gives the conscious one a strength comparable to an obsession; the obsessiveness can produce outcomes such as achievements of special perfection or resistance in the face of opposition. In the more usual course of events, however, unconscious impulses make their way into consciousness through loosely associated ideas, which, on account of their dissimilarity with the original ones, evade the censor that would otherwise keep them out; an instance would be the earlier example in which a woman, unaware (let us assume) of her growing passion for a man who enjoys picking blueberries, takes on that or a similar pastime herself. Derivative impulses, such as that, as Freud calls them, continue in fantasy and ultimately substitute formations and symptoms.

The conscious, meanwhile, acts on the unconscious in ways other than by adding to the unconscious by means of the repression of unwanted impulses. Treatment by psychoanalysis is predicated on this possibility, that conscious processes can influence unconscious ones, even if slowly and laboriously. Patients in analysis reach gingerly back through the so-called derivatives of the unconscious that remain accessible to consciousness in order to meet and disarm the resistances blocking off the unconscious impulses.

It is in pathology that the most striking interpenetration of unconscious and conscious occurs. We are already familiar with the symptoms of psychoneurosis, like Anna O.'s inability to drink, that show a corruption of conscious function by repressed impulses that have made their way forward through derivatives; they lock into place because the original impulse remains repressed. But it is in the narcissistic disorders, like schizophrenia, that the intrusion of the unconscious into the conscious manifests most clearly.

These are the disorders in which sufferers do not retain a love object even in fantasy and therefore, according to Freud, prove inaccessible to psychoanalytic therapy, which requires transference of such a relationship onto the practitioner (see Chapter 4 here). Whereas that relationship makes possible the gradual coaxing of unconscious ideas into consciousness in the treatment of psychoneurotics, no such option exists in the treatment of schizophrenics. However, as Freud and his colleagues discovered, those patients make the connection between conscious and unconscious themselves, only abstractly, through their speech or their bodily organs.

One patient, for example, who had quarreled with her lover, felt her eyes were not right, they were *twisted*. She herself explained the derivation: she could not understand him, he always looked different; he was a hypocrite, an eye-twister – the German *Augenverdreher* means "deceiver" figuratively; he had twisted her eyes; now she had twisted eyes; they were no longer her eyes, and she was seeing the world through different eyes. The patient's eyes took over the whole of her disparagement of her lover, concentrating all the relevant thoughts into the sensation of one organ and the verbal reference to it.[7]

Freud, based on instances like that of the packaging of entire unconscious complexes into speech, extracts the hypothesis that

---

[7]   Freud draws the example from Viktor Tausk (Freud 1915c, pp. 197–198).

thought in general may make its way into the preconscious and conscious by becoming encoded in language. Thought, which he presumes to begin in the unconscious, is lifted to consciousness when transformed into a medium – language – that secondary-process thinking can assimilate.

8　Beyond the pleasure principle: *Beyond the Pleasure Principle* (1920)

> Enough is left unexplained to justify the hypothesis of a compulsion to repeat – something that seems more primitive, more elementary, more instinctual, than the pleasure principle which it overrides.
>
> – S. Freud, *Beyond the Pleasure Principle*, 1920, p. 23.

Freud's 1920 monograph Beyond the Pleasure Principle *marks a turning point in his idea of the most basic forces governing mental life. In it he asserts the existence of a genuine exception to the pleasure principle that he regards as sufficiently far-reaching to require a restructuring of the theory.*

The exception consists of people's compulsive repetition of previous experiences in the absence of any evident payoff: when people return repeatedly to horrific moments of their lives, as soldiers with post-traumatic stress disorder might do in recurrently dreaming a catastrophic shelling in the trenches, they bring on an experience with no redeeming value, according to Freud. Called the repetition compulsion, the tendency toward these repetitions can override the pleasure principle.

Freud extrapolates from the repetition compulsion to the existence of a death instinct, a trend toward quiescence and dissolution present in all living things: life first arose from inorganic material, and individual living entities return to that state at death. Death and inorganicity also represent the complete absence of stimulation; individuals verge on returning to that state on a smaller scale insofar as they strive toward the reduction of stimulation, the aim expressed by the pleasure principle and what Freud will present as its refinements.

Finally, introducing a new dualism as the overarching dynamic of mental life, Freud conceives the death instinct as operating in

opposition to the life instincts, which by the end of the monograph
subsume both the sexual and ego instincts of his former schematic.
The sexual and ego instincts, although thus grouped together, retain
the potential for conflict Freud previously observed them to have (see
Chapter 5).

This work is, by Freud's own admission, one of his most spec-
ulative and far-fetched, especially the portion in which he derives and
then justifies the death instinct and posits some of its consequences;
the narrative is one of his most obscure. But psychological insight and
intriguing turns of argument abound in its pages, which repay patient
attention.

THE REPETITION COMPULSION

Freud found in the dreams of *traumatic neurotics*, those suffering
from what we know today as post-traumatic stress disorder, a characteristic that supersedes the pleasure principle. That distinguishing
characteristic is the repeated return to the scene of the trauma and its
evocation of terror, but without the presumptive payoff latent in
ordinary nightmares; in the ordinary nightmare we may be punishing
ourselves for the dream – for fulfillment of a wish otherwise repu-
diated – or disguising the wish's fulfillment to avoid its detection by
the sleeping ego (1900, Ch. 7, Section C).

Dreams, Freud had argued since *The Interpretation of Dreams*
(1900), are supposed to fulfill wishes and in so doing conform to the
pleasure principle. But patients suffering from traumatic neuroses
gain no such benefit from their dreams, and no amount of repetition
of the dream lessens the fright they experience. So, Freud concludes,
either dreams do not at bottom serve the function of wish-fulfillment,
or traumatic neurosis somehow upsets that function.[1]

---

[1]   Or, he suggests in a line added in a later edition of the text, the dreams express
masochistic trends in the ego of unknown origin. The origin of the masochism, if
masochism indeed intervenes, remains mysterious insofar as we cannot attribute the
self-assault to any obvious instigator like survivor guilt. Traumatic neurosis, with its
accompanying recurrent dreams, can arise in people around whom no one else has died.

Preparatory to resolving the question, Freud examines other contexts in which people repeat painful past events to see whether they, too, stretch the limits of the pleasure principle.

For one example, children from an early age re-enact in their play events that distressed them when they occurred. In a signature vignette, Freud describes an 18-month-old boy's practice of throwing small objects into hard-to-reach places and, with an expression of satisfaction, declaring them, *"fort,"* the German word for "gone"; sometimes he would retrieve the objects himself with an expression of joy, or *"da"* ("there"). Freud and the child's mother discerned that the boy was re-enacting the mother's intermittent departures, which he can only have found distressing. Freud extrapolates that the child was turning an event outside his control into one under his control: he determined when his mother would and would not go, and he might also have been expressing his defiance, as if saying, "Go away! See if I care!" (Freud, 1920, pp. 14–16).

In general, Freud says, children repeat in their play everything that has made an impression on them. They thereby reduce it to manageable size and, as they do with negative experiences, gain control over it; at the same time, they can have a forum for expressing one of the dominant wishes of childhood, to be big and grown-up. Thus, insofar as children achieve relief and pleasure from incorporating the repetition of painful events into their play, the repetition yields easily to explanation by the pleasure principle.

The psychoanalytic process produces a different context in which people repeat painful events, in this case with less evident payoff: patients experience *transference* onto the therapist of repressed impulses and impressions deriving from their early relationships with their primary others. Patients may project onto their therapists, alongside positive attributes of their earlier relationships like warmth and protectiveness, negative experiences, like the perception of scorn and the sense of abandonment. Particularly painful in the latter regard are the feelings of failure and loss of love that accompany the end of infantile sexual life as children's strivings for the parent of the opposite gender conclude in disappointment; to those may be added jealousy and feelings of betrayal if a new baby joins the household. That constellation of feelings in turn resolves into a narcissistic scar consisting of a permanent compromising of self-regard and sense of inferiority.

Patients perceive the same frustrations and disappointments in their relationship with the therapist. They contrive to feel scorned and inadequate and to find objects of jealousy, and may accordingly attempt to terminate treatment when it has only half begun. All these perceptions, Freud says, reflect only impulses, long repressed, attempting to reach satisfaction by means of repetition. But, important for the discussion of the pleasure principle, revival of the impulses leads only to unpleasure as it did in the past. Repetition of the repressed impulses must therefore be the result of a compulsion, which is definable as an imperative that ignores the absence of any payoff.

A similar compulsion to repeat earlier painful experiences sometimes arises in the lives of healthy people. Freud calls the pattern a *compulsion of destiny*, citing as examples those whose close friendships seem always to end in betrayal, benefactors whose protégés seem always to abandon them in anger, individuals whose succession of love affairs pass through the same phases as the ones before them and end the same way.

These examples of repeated life events of both healthy and neurotic people seem to bespeak a compulsion to repeat that exceeds the pleasure principle. Yet we would have difficulty even in these cases identifying repetition that excludes the pleasure principle. Even the most devastating transference experiences may serve patients' self-punitive impulses and, with or without that motive, can be exploited toward a cure. In the achievement of the unknowing repetition in transference alone, repressed impulses gain at least partial expression, as they also do when brought forth in therapy as denials (see Chapter 6).[2] Therapist and patient can use the emerging

---

[2]   For the repressed material to have encroached this closely upon consciousness, Freud surmises, the work of treatment must have already loosened the repression to some degree. Freud adds in a footnote that patients' submissive stance toward the doctor may

material to help the patient remember rather than repeat these experiences, so as to be able to perceive them as the memories they are as opposed to as the current reality they appear to be. In the compulsion of destiny as well, when life experiences seem to repeat over and over again, the repetitions may answer a need of some kind, such that people bring them about in some way; for example, the betrayed friend may subtly cultivate the serial betrayals, which answer the need to feel worthless at the hands of an historical other.

The dreams of traumatic neurotics present the clearest case of a pure compulsion to repeat, Freud thinks. He can identify no urge, other than the compulsion itself, the repetition might satisfy. But even in the other cases, in which some payoff can be detected – in children's play, for example, or transference in therapy – Freud perceives a repetition that exceeds the payoff and thus goes beyond the attainment of pleasure. He sees something more elemental and "instinctual" (Freud, 1920, p. 23), by which he appears to mean something involuntary and driven as though in someone possessed.

Freud now believes a compulsion to repeat exists that must be more fundamental than the pleasure principle and so can override it. He devotes the remainder of *Beyond the Pleasure Principle* to his admittedly speculative expansion on this imperative, including its origin and its implications for the major forces governing mental life. He is following a train of thought to its logical conclusion and doing so more out of the intellectual passion he calls curiosity than out of conviction. Readers are well advised to bear that – Freud's own – caveat in mind so as to extract the account's psychological insights and avoid becoming waylaid by its stretched plausibility. In the course of the discussion he does no less than revise his conception of the fundaments of the mind.

> dispose them toward the repetition, which is to say the transference. Patients fall naturally into the submissive stance in treatment on account of the activation of their unconscious parental complexes. They have the all-knowing doctor, viz. authority figure, on the one hand, and the ignorant and perhaps naughty child – themselves, as the patient – on the other.

THE GENESIS AND DYNAMICS OF THE REPETITION COMPULSION

In an attempt to elucidate the conditions that propagate the repetition compulsion, Freud examines the impact of trauma, the producer of the clearest instances of the compulsion, on the workings of the mind.

He anchors the examination in an anatomically inspired view of the origin of consciousness, which, he says, arises in the mind's outermost layer and serves the purpose of shielding the inner layers from stimuli. That outermost layer receives all stimuli and acts as a barrier through which only some excitations pass to the inner layers, which are able to act on and store them. Freud speculates, perhaps fancifully, that this outermost layer of the mind became permanently modified in our evolutionary history precisely because of the constant bombardment of stimuli on it.[3]

Freud defines any stimulus from the outside that has the strength to break through the protective shield as *traumatic*. An event of this kind produces a massive disturbance in the organism's energy and arouses all its defenses. The pleasure principle cannot function in this environment. Nothing can prevent the mind from becoming overrun by stimuli, the onslaught of stimuli necessarily being a source of unpleasure. The mind needs to master and bind, or contain, the stimuli[4] before it can discharge them in accordance with the pleasure principle. Thus in the case of trauma, the pleasure principle is preempted by a more urgent necessity, to gain control of the stimuli so the mind has the option of discharging them.[5]

---

[3]   That permanent modification left the mind's outer layer in a state, described by Freud as "baked through" (Freud, 1920, p. 26), on account of which it became adept at registering excitation, but could undergo no further modification itself. Having become "baked through" and hence brittle, it could not retain or alter stimuli, either of those operations entailing a change in the substance in which the operation takes place. Those operations – remembering and thinking, respectively – were left to the mind's inner layers. This conception generally restates Freud's previously articulated image of the conscious as a purely receptive organ (see Chapter 7 here).

[4]   See Chapter 7 for a definition of Freud's concept of binding.

[5]   Freud uses the same template to explain the specific unpleasure of physical pain. That experience, he suggests, may result from a breach in the protective shield that extends

It is the binding of stimuli the mind lacks the preparation to undertake. This is the essence of fright, which seems to be present whenever a traumatic neurosis materializes (Freud, 1920, p. 12). The lack of preparation means the systems that would first receive the stimuli are not on alert and so are easily overrun. Anxiety, by contrast with fright, is the state of vigilance that anticipates a fearsome event and thus affords a buffer against the event's impact. It rouses the relevant systems, which can then bind the invading stimuli.

The recurrent, unforgiving dreams of traumatic neurotics, Freud surmises, may generate anxiety after the fact, as though to set up the protective barrier that was missing when the traumatic event occurred. The mind is trying to master the stimulus retrospectively by returning to the originating scene with an expectation of preparedness and, as we know, failing miserably. Freud posits this attempted mastery of stimuli as the older function of dreams, older than the fulfillment of wishes. Dreams cannot take up the fulfillment of wishes until the mental apparatus is able to stop its flow of excitations from leaking.

This account of traumatic neurosis can explain a further feature of the disorder Freud and his contemporaries noted: that physical injury at the time of combat trauma did not necessarily increase the odds of developing war neurosis. A soldier who was gravely wounded in the trenches was no more likely to develop traumatic neurosis than the compatriot next to him who was not. Physical injury provides a stimulation of its own that largely overrides other potential sources of agitation, like the fright occasioned by the absence of anticipation. The stimulation afforded by mechanical agitation on the body, even if painful, traces to the capacity of any such disturbance to produce sexual excitation (see Chapter 4). Physical illness can have the same

to a limited area. The breach occasions what Freud describes as a continuous stream of excitation flowing from the site of the injury to the central part of the mind. Normally this kind of flow would arise from within the organism. Stimuli that originate externally usually impact the organism in a more discrete fashion. The mind responds to the invasion by summoning energy to the breach and away from all other areas, effectively paralyzing them.

effect, such that even severe psychopathologies such as melancholia (depression) and schizophrenia can undergo temporary remission when a patient becomes physically sick.[6]

Although consciousness, or the outermost cortical layer that will become consciousness, may shield the mind from stimuli from without, it offers no such protection against stimuli arising from within. Those stimuli are indexed by feelings of pleasure and unpleasure – we find them agreeable or we dread them – and as such they take precedence over all others, given the potency of pleasure and unpleasure in the workings of the mind.[7] Without protection against them, stimuli arising from within have an even greater capacity to induce trauma than do external stimuli. The former – impulses arising from the instincts, like forbidden lust for Dad or murderous impulses toward him – arise from the unconscious portion of the mind, where unconstrained, or "unbound," energy flows.

The higher strata of the mind, including discursive thought and reason, have the task of binding, or reducing and containing, that energy. When those higher processes cannot accomplish that task, the instinctual impulse produces a disturbance, a release of vast pools of energy in the mind, akin to a traumatic neurosis. The mind will adopt as its first task the containment – "binding" – of that energy. That effort, manifesting in the compulsion to repeat so as to (retroactively) anticipate the onslaught of stimuli, will once again put the pleasure principle out of action until such a time as the binding occurs.

In thus acting in disregard of the pleasure principle, the behavior produced by the compulsion to repeat looks instinctual in character,

---

[6]   Although the weight of contemporary clinical evidence suggests physical injury might exacerbate the chances of developing a traumatic neurosis, now called PTSD (e.g., Dyster-Aas *et al.*, 2012; Koren *et al.*, 2005; but see also Sijbrandij *et al.*, 2013), Freud's remarks here are noteworthy for their suggestion of a dynamic that could arise in traumatic disorder and does arise in other contexts.

[7]   One result of that primacy, as we have seen, is that when internal excitations produce excessive unpleasure, the mind treats them as though they were emanating from the outside. Via the mechanism of *projection*, we tend to deflect outward those sources of disquiet that come from the self but from which we cannot escape. Once we perceive those sources as emanating from outside us we can avert them.

Freud observes. The behavior appears driven by an automatism unrelated to the outcome of the act in progress; it gives the impression of being driven by a demonic force when it runs contrary to the pleasure principle – when, that is, the repetition brings only pain and distress (Freud, 1920, p. 35). Children's play is an exception. Children repeat experiences, unpleasurable as well as pleasurable, to master and become an active agent of them, the repetitions thus serving a positive purpose and in doing so conforming to the pleasure principle. They do not appear mechanical, whereas the hapless repetitions experienced by traumatic neurotics in their dreams, by patients in psychoanalysis undergoing transference of their painful childhood relationships, and by adults trapped in the "compulsion of destiny" appear otherwise.

THE REPETITION COMPULSION AND INSTINCT

Freud begins to suspect that if compulsively repetitive behavior operating in total disregard of its effects looks instinctual – like a recurrent dream that returns a soldier to the horror of the trenches – then a connection might exist between compulsive repetition and instinct. And instincts do, in fact, repeat something. The hunger instinct presses us to attain satiety every time the instinct manifests. When satisfied, the instinct restores the organism to the state it was in – with respect to hunger – before the tension arising from the instinct mounted.

Now, Freud continues, launching the decidedly speculative discussion that will occupy the rest of his essay, if instincts, which form the basic building blocks of mental life, inherently drive toward repetition, then perhaps organic life – the life of all living things – does this in general. An urge may exist in organic life to restore an earlier state of things (Freud, 1920, p. 36). Freud cites the migration of birds and the spawning of fish as examples on a large scale of this impulsion (Freud, 1920, p. 37). Freud's discussion, as tracked here, shifts somewhat erratically between the individual and species as the referent of the trend toward repetition. That erratic trajectory does not diminish

Freud's earlier more careful and more empirically grounded case for a trend toward repetition in the individual psyche.

However, if life is inertial, then some other force must prod it to leave its initial state, toward which it presses to return thereafter. That disturbing force, Freud reasons, must come from the outside. Thus, the proposition emerges that all instincts, and life in general, seek to restore an earlier state of things they were forced to abandon by external disturbing processes.

But now Freud faces an apparent contradiction among his claims. If, as he has just concluded, external influences are what disturb the initial state organic instincts seek to restore, then this is to say that external influences provoke the phenomena of *development* (Freud, 1920, p. 380). Earlier he had said the opposite – that instincts, and not external stimuli, bring development about (1915a; see Chapter 5 here). According to the new analysis, instinctual action could not provoke development, because it only reproduces a prior state.

Nonetheless, he continues, the new view accommodates the old one. He contended earlier that instinctual stimuli, like hunger pangs, force the development of the mind because the organism cannot satisfy the need created by such stimuli by reflexive means; it cannot withdraw from an internal irritant. It must recruit the means to bring about satisfaction and hence must develop those means. According to the new view of instincts as inherently conservative, irritants, whether internal or external, propel an instinct into action, while the instinct in itself only presses toward a restoration of the previous state. In necessitating the creation of the means to bring that restoration about, the instinct, or more precisely the need created by the instinct, also acts as a "disturbing" influence that, like external experience, can bring about development. The organism, having been forced to change by disturbing influences, would store each modification for later repetition, Freud says. Thus life would evolve, though not through any intrinsic aim of the instincts.

THE DEATH INSTINCT

If the instincts, and hence life in general, ultimately seek to restore earlier states, then, Freud says, life cannot have as its goal a state of things it has not yet attained. It must aim toward an old state, from which it departed under force of necessity. The original state from which life emerged was inorganic. Life, then, must observe an imperative to return to inorganicity. To be inorganic is to be dead. It follows that the aim of all life has to be death; there is a *death instinct*. This is the controversial, and as Freud warned, far-fetched, conclusion of this work.

In keeping with that conclusion, some as-yet unknown process would have to have triggered life in inorganic matter initially. That unknown process would have produced a tension in the substance, having disturbed its original state to which it would press to return. That press, in turn, would have formed the first instinct; the instinct would have had the aim of returning the organism to its original, inorganic state, much as the tension in a stretched rubber band "aims" to return the rubber band to its original form. The organism would have found it easy to make this return at first, Freud extrapolates, but external influences, as just discussed, would have forced it on an ever-widening detour from that path. Those influences would have forced the organism to accommodate in some way, and each accommodation would have been stored up for later repetition, the accommodations gradually altering the organism.

At first glance the instincts of self-preservation, mastery, and self-assertion, all part of what Freud calls the ego, or self-preservative, instincts (see Chapter 5), would seem to contradict the death instinct: we avoid threats to life and limb; we attempt to gain control of that which would defeat us; and we put our interests forward. Freud says that, no, these impulses only assure that the organism follows its own path to death so that it may die through decay rather than by external accident. Nonetheless, the paradox remains that the organism strives most vigorously against those events that would hasten its life's aim, namely to die. But that impression conforms absolutely to the program of the instincts: they persist in their aim no matter what the circumstances. We strive to satisfy our self-preservative instinct – to feed ourselves when we are hungry, to dodge an oncoming truck, etc. – even if we also have an instinct to let ourselves expire, i.e., a death instinct; conversely, we will continue to trend toward expiration even though we aim instinctively to stay alive.[8]

THE LIFE INSTINCTS

Freud, unconvinced thus far of the incompatibility of the self-preservative (ego) instincts and the death instinct, finds a clearer opposition between the sexual instincts and the death instinct. The sexual instincts bring us together with another human being and from that union produce new life. The combination of entities into greater unities and the perpetuation of life through the creation of new life – these results contrast with the idea of destruction, or the coming apart of things, which aligns more naturally with death and decay.

The sexual instincts are therefore the instincts of life, or the *life instincts*. They have the task of watching over and protecting the elementary entities that must separate from the individual and meet with other germ cells to ignite new life. In the light of their ultimate aim toward union, Freud compares them with the *Eros* of classical poets, which on his reading designates the force that holds all living things together (Freud, 1920, p. 50).

Freud insists that no instincts, aside from the sexual ones, create new forms; as instincts they only press toward the restoration of an earlier state. Thus, he believes, no instinct exists toward higher development in the animal or plant world. He proposes that what appear to us in human or societal development as intellectual and cultural advances may arise from the sequelae of repression: repressed instincts continue to strive for satisfaction and find it through substitute formations, or they may become sublimated instead of

---

[8] Freud shortly alters his view regarding the categorization of the ego instincts (see two sections hence, "The life and death instincts").

repressed. But the latter processes allow only partial expression of the original instinct, which will therefore continue to strive for satisfaction in whatever direction growth remains open to it. Those processes would account for the impression of the creation of ever-new forms.[9]

THE LIFE AND DEATH INSTINCTS

Freud stresses the dualism of the view he has elaborated: as one group of instincts rushes toward the final aim of life in death, the other jerks the process back to make a fresh start, the sexual instincts emblematic of the latter group (Freud, 1920, pp. 40–41). He finds support even in our remote biological origins for his idea that these two fundamental thrusts exist in living things, one toward life, or construction, and one toward death, or destruction: the sexual instincts, as the force that pushes life back to its starting point, could have operated from the outset of life, before the sexes differentiated. After addressing some biological evidence that death may have arisen later in evolution than reproduction, which would make any instinct toward death derivative, Freud concludes the death instinct is primordial too.[10] He finds philosophical echoes of the dualism in Schopenhauer's conception

---

[9]   Freud (1910) elaborated as an example of the process Leonardo's thirst for scientific knowledge.

[10]   Experiments apparently producing indefinite life in unicellular organisms seem initially to suggest a delayed appearance of death in evolution and thus to invalidate Freud's claim of the primacy of the death instinct. However, the researchers turn out to have kept their organisms alive by repeatedly replacing the fluid in which the organisms lived. Left to their own devices they would have died from the refuse of their vital processes. A separate investigation demonstrated, however, that weakening Protista could be revived through conjugation with other cells. Freud believes the latter demonstration supports his designation of the combination of substances into ever greater wholes as the origin and essence of the life instincts (Woodruff (1914); Lipschütz (1914); Weismann (1884, p. 84f); Freud (1920, pp. 46–47, pp. 49–50); Hering (1878, p. 77ff)).

The same dualism finds expression in other work. Weismann (1884, p. 84f, Freud, 1920, p. 319) distinguished between the germ-plasm of multi-cellular organisms, which perpetuates life upon conjugation with other germ-plasm, and the soma, or individual body, which becomes expendable upon the conjugation (Freud, 1920, p. 50). Hering (1878, p. 77ff) claimed the existence of two opposing processes constantly at work in living matter, one constructive and the other destructive.

that death is the result and to that extent the purpose of life, and the sexual instincts embody the will to live (Freud, 1920, p. 50).

But now Freud realizes the sexual instincts may not be the only constituent of the life instincts. The ego instincts may, after all, fit in that category as well. The libido, or the energy of the sexual instincts, can take the ego as object. Thus, he envisions, the libido is originally pooled in the ego, or what will become the ego, and is only gradually drawn away from there and directed toward external objects, some of it always remaining behind in the ego (Freud, 1914; see Chapter 4). Freud ventures, extrapolating from that argument, that because the ego is invested with libido, then the instincts that protect and nurture the ego must likewise express libido. Accordingly, the ego instincts, as expressions of, but still distinct from, the sexual instincts, must support the perpetuation of life, not the trend toward death. They are therefore properly classed as life instincts.

Although both the sexual and ego instincts express the life instincts, some opposition remains between them, Freud continues to think, insofar as they may conflict; they still represent the potentially competing interests of sexuality and self-preservation, or love and necessity. The etiology of the psychoneuroses attests to these conflicts, for instance in pointing to the strife between erotic urges toward a parent and the fear of annihilation such urges might arouse.

Freud concedes that further investigation might eventually reveal ego instincts that are not libidinally tinged, in which case the affiliation he initially conceived between the ego and death instincts may hold in part. As of this writing, however, and in later ones (see Chapter 11), he sees only ego instincts with libidinal coloration. He warns us, however, not to confuse that overlap with the idea that a single, ubiquitous energy governs all of mental life.[11] At a minimum, the sexual and ego instincts, which together comprise the life instincts, oppose the death instincts, which Freud envisions as expressing a separate energy. Our mental life is fundamentally dualistic, he

---

[11]   Freud took pains to disavow the latter idea, a view associated with C.G. Jung.

believes; it is a tapestry of different interests that sometimes conflict, sometimes strive in disregard of one another, and sometimes align.

EVIDENCE OF THE DEATH INSTINCT

The death instinct works silently by its nature, Freud says, and therefore lends itself less easily than the life instincts do to observation. Nonetheless, he points to what he thinks are two manifestations of it.

The first is sadism, which Freud originally conceived as part of the sexual instinct and now thinks could not, with its aim to injure the object, emanate from Eros, whose aim is to preserve life. He envisions instead a genesis of sadism from the death instinct, which, along with the life instincts, inhabits the primitive ego. The death instinct, left to its own devices, would insure the organism's drift toward disintegration and death. But the life instincts expel it outward, where it becomes visible as destructive action against the love objects the individual eventually establishes there. Thus rechanneled, the death instinct, now as sadism, is put in service of the sexual function, for instance, in the effort to control and dominate the object.

This new vision of sadism occasions a revision of Freud's original conception of how the vicissitude of sadism–masochism unfolds (1915a; see Chapter 5). According to the original view, the sequence begins with sadism, in the form of efforts to dominate the object though without any intent to hurt it. In anticipation of negative repercussions from the environment, we turn the trend inward and direct it against the self, thus introducing masochism. Once we turn our destructiveness toward ourselves, we experience the pain it can inflict, along with the arousal the pain brings (see Chapter 4, also Chapter 10, below). The arousal experienced, we turn the trend around again, back to sadism, and assault the object with the intent specifically of producing pain and its arousal, which we enjoy vicariously. Now that the trend has a subject (the individual), an object (the external other), and an intended effect (the pain), the trend may reverse yet again, from "active" to "passive" (Freud, 1915a; Chapter 5 here) such that individuals – now as object – seek to suffer at the hand of a specific other.

Under the new view, which posits an original state containing a death instinct within, masochism would have to embody the first manifestation of the polarity sadism–masochism, in the form of a tendency toward dissolution. The life instincts, simultaneously operative, would, in acting to preserve the self, bring about the expulsion of the death instinct from the self, producing outward-directed destructiveness, or primitive sadism. The rest of the sequence Freud originally outlined would follow from there, with the difference that the first turning around of sadism toward the self would produce secondary masochism, rather than the first-ever occurrence of the tendency (1920, pp. 55–56).

The second line of evidence Freud cites for the operation of a death instinct may be found in, of all places, the pleasure principle, or as he now says, its close affiliate, the *nirvana principle*.[12] The dominant tendency of individual mental life, and perhaps of nervous life in general, is to reduce, keep constant, or remove internal tension that arises on account of stimuli. Although until now this tendency has defined the pleasure principle, Freud begins to allow that pleasure may arise in other ways as well, a theme he will develop shortly in other works (e.g., 1924; see Chapter 10 here). Thus, henceforth he will use "nirvana principle" to refer to the tendency specifically toward quiescence, whereby we seek a reduction, and ultimately elimination, of stimulation.[13]

The intersection between that tendency and the death instinct resides in the definition of death as the complete removal of all stimulation. This is not to say we want to die every time we want to eliminate stimuli, rather that the release we achieve resembles the release of death and thus expresses a similar tendency. It is in the light of this affinity that Freud believes the observations confirming the nirvana/pleasure principle afford evidence also of a death instinct.

[12]   After Low (1920, p. 56).

[13]   He also, as of this writing, acknowledges the close association between the nirvana and pleasure principles and the *constancy principle* of the psychophysicist G.T. Fechner (1873), according to which mental life strives to keep quantities of excitation as low as possible or at least constant.

Now that the convergence of the death instinct with stimulus reduction is established, the stage is set for the ongoing interchange between the two classes of instinct: The life instincts introduce tensions, which the death instinct leads the organism to eliminate; the life instincts introduce fresh tensions, etc.. Within the compass of the life instincts, the sexual instincts in particular not only create new life, they also, in some cases, breathe fresh life into the mating organism: Freud cites the finding that weakened single-cell organisms rejuvenate when they coalesce.[14]

PASSIVITY OF THE DEATH INSTINCT

Freud is clear in the foregoing that the death instinct is passive, as of this writing, in that it represents the drift toward complete quiescence, ultimately inorganicity; hence its convergence with the pleasure/nirvana principle, insofar as that principle expresses the urge in mental life toward the discharge of stimulation, or tension.

In that light, it is important to distinguish the death instinct from aggression, which involves an active exertion. Despite the prominence Freud accords aggression in his later works (e.g., 1930; Chapters 9, 10, and 11 here), he consistently conceived it as derivative of the death instinct (e.g., 1940a; Chapters 9, 11, and Epilogue here). At this juncture, he extrapolates the beginning of that view. If, as he has concluded, the death instinct, like the life instincts, operates in the organism from the first, and the organism does not die immediately, then something must be keeping it alive. He conjectures that the life instincts neutralize the drift toward death, by expelling impulses in that direction from the ego toward the outside world. Freud addresses how that transformation takes place in subsequent works (see Chapters 9–11).

---

[14]   Lipschütz, 1914, in Freud, 1920 p. 47 and 55. See also Note 11, this chapter. In follow-up work scientists produced the same result when they injected a single organism with chemical or mechanical stimuli in lieu of having it join with a second organism (Lipschütz, 1914). Freud sees this as additional support for the idea that coalescence mimics the introduction of fresh stimulus, or new chemical tensions.

THE LIFE AND DEATH INSTINCTS AND THE REPETITION
COMPULSION

Whereas the death instinct easily manifests a compulsion to repeat, Freud finds it difficult to identify an equivalent compulsion among the life instincts. The death instinct returns living substance to the inorganic state that preceded life; in the shorter term it returns the organism beset by stimuli to its quiescent state – hungry babies, once fed, calm down, for example. In the life instincts, he finds only an incidental repetition of something old: sexual union, which begins a new life, repeats a result – the creation of life – that occurred at the start of life historically (1920, p. 55). That analogy, however, contains no representation of the act of coalescence that produces the life in complex organisms and toward which the sexual instincts prod us.

All Freud can do to fill the resulting lacuna is point whimsically to the metaphor provided by the myth ascribed to Aristophanes in Plato's *Symposium*. Originally man and woman existed as a double individual. The combined man–woman, subsequently cut in two by Zeus, strives to return to one. Recurring to the start of life on earth, Freud supposes that living substance, at its inception, became rent into small particles, which since then have striven to reunite.

Freud closes the volume, whose speculative nature he again emphasizes, with a reminder that the compulsion to repeat does not so much contradict the pleasure principle as lie outside it. The repetition compulsion performs the function of containing and channeling the uncontrolled energy that comes from stimuli impinging on the mind, especially those stimuli that overwhelm, like instinctual impulses. In this exercise of containing, or binding, it must disregard its generation of unpleasure. The repetition that brings about that unpleasure may revive decided pain. But the result will ready the excitation for discharge and thus ultimately bring about the generation of pleasure for which the individual has never given up striving (pp. 62–63).

9   A new architecture of the mind: *The Ego and the Id* (1923)

> We have formed the idea that in each individual there is a coherent organization of mental processes; and we call this his *ego*. It is to this ego that consciousness is attached .... We have come upon something in the ego ... which is also unconscious.

– S. Freud, *The Ego and the Id*, p. 17.

In The Ego and the Id *Freud systematizes the conceptualization of the mind's architecture that has evolved steadily through his works and for which he is best known, the tripartite schema of id, ego, and superego. The id comprises our unmediated impulses, the ego our judging and thinking self, and the superego our conscience. Freud develops the justification for his shift to this conceptualization, details its constituents, and explores further, now in distinctly psychological terms, the dualism of the life and death instincts introduced in* Beyond the Pleasure Principle *(see Chapter 8 here). The Ego and the Id hews more closely to clinical observation and leaves biology aside. It drives all the works that follow it.*

The most course-changing contribution of The Ego and the Id *beyond the new structural vocabulary is Freud's delineation of the superego. Humans, according to Freud's conception, develop a self-monitor concerned specifically with propriety. The process evolves in part in response to the differentiation from the parents and its attendant ambivalence. We want our autonomy and must grow away from the parents; at the same time, we wish to continue their embrace and protection. Installing an internal version of them – forming a superego – accomplishes both of these aims: we gain our independence from them, and we keep them with us. Were the superego born solely of this dynamic, it would have an enveloping and softening character. Instead we have a harsh critic and judge. Freud spends much of the latter part of the book attempting to account for that discrepancy.*

A NEW STRUCTURAL TAXONOMY

The Ego and the Id begins with a demonstration of the inadequacy of the structural division of the mind into conscious and unconscious portions (see Chapter 7) in providing full account of the mind's dynamics: both the impulses we repress and the forces that lead us to repress them and "resist" their re-emergence are unconscious. A system that distinguishes only unconscious and conscious processes cannot characterize that opposition. Nor can it provide a basis for identifying the impetus to repress – the judgment by some area of the mind that an idea is dangerous, such that the operations to keep it from becoming conscious come into play. Freud, recognizing these problems, makes way for their solution by offering a new taxonomic division of the mind, id, ego, and super-ego. He reminds us not to conceive these too literally. Although he refers to them as agencies, they have no physical reality; they denote different forces within the mind.

> *Id* represents our unconscious impulses, both inherited and repressed, as they arise naturally, untainted by any external influences; in common parlance it consists of our passions (Freud, 1923, p. 25).
>
> *Ego* operates both consciously and unconsciously: it embodies people's strivings to avert danger, whether from internal or external sources, and to maintain their bearings in the environment; it includes judgment, reasoning, and negation, the elements of rational thinking and common sense (Freud, 1923, p. 25).
>
> *Superego*, a differentiation that arises within the ego, observes the ego and judges it. Although its judging function may make it seem rational and thus aligned with the ego, the judgments arise instantly and unthinkingly, driven, as Freud will decide, by impulses in the id (Freud, 1923, p. 28ff).

ID AND EGO

Freud says little of the id here, having encompassed it in his earlier treatment of the repressed unconscious (see Chapters 2 and 7 here).

The ego, his primary concern early in *The Ego and the Id*, forms from the id, which consists only of impulses seeking discharge and where the pleasure principle reigns exclusively. An organism that seeks only to discharge its impulses cannot fulfill its needs; hence we modify our impulses by taking account of our experience in the external world. We thus observe the reality, as well as the pleasure, principle. Whereas the pleasure principle would allow us to satisfy a need such as hunger by mere hallucination, the reality principle prompts us to eat; it ensures our lasting satisfaction and moves us to monitor the external environment to that end (see Chapter 2 here).

Freud labels as ego the latter embodiment of our impulses as they are influenced by our experience in the external world. The ego encompasses what Freud calls our *percept-consciousness*, and he conceives the constituent links – perceptions including awareness of our body, along with words and memories – as its nucleus. The ego also subsumes our preconscious thought and some unconscious judgments, including our censorship of unwanted unconscious impulses and the resistances by means of which we keep those impulses at bay. The ego of Freud's system approximates the entity we would call the self in lay parlance, the individual we refer to when we say "I."

Despite its status as the seat of consciousness and rationality, Freud's ego plays a passive role in life. Freud conceived it as "'lived'" by unknown and uncontrollable forces, the latter emanating from the id, and ultimately the superego (Freud, 1923, p. 23).[1] It serves as a way-station, a transmitter and filter of other forces, as opposed to the colorful seat of action lay conceptions might associate with it.

---

[1]   Freud credits Georg Groddeck (1923), a contemporary who emphasized the psychosomatic in mental life, with the inspiration for this idea. He also adopted the term *id* from Groddeck, who, Freud assumes, followed Nietzsche's use of the term for the impersonal part of our nature, which observes natural law as opposed to our will.

Freud mentions some tendencies of the mind that do not fall easily within the functions of the ego or the id. Self-criticism and conscience, which we normally associate with higher mental function and hence with the ego, sometimes operate unconsciously and with apparent irrationality. Although those features suggest an association with the id, judgment of any sort, let alone of ourselves, falls distinctly outside the purview of the id. Thus emerges the postulation of a third entity, the superego, formerly referred to by Freud as the ego-ideal (1914; see Chapter 4 here).

THE SUPEREGO

The term superego stands for the judgments we pass, largely unawares, on our own impulses, acts, and thoughts. Those judgments, in response to which we feel remorse or guilt and inhibit our behavior, can have a harsh, punishing quality. Although we fear them and strive to behave so as to avert them, again largely outside awareness, we may consciously experience their weight in the form of general malaise or, in more extreme cases, depression.

According to Freud, the superego evolves from the Oedipal conflict that arises in the normal development of every individual (see Chapters 1, 6, and 7 here). In its simple version it unfolds as follows, for boys. Boys yearn first for their mother and later also identify with their father, once they have populated their environment with distinct others. As their desires for their mother grow more intense, they perceive their father as an obstacle and want to eliminate and replace him. But because they also wish to possess the father's privileges, they wish to be like him; therefore they continue to identify with him amidst the enmity they also feel. The relationship thus becomes ambivalent, in that boys want both to take the father into the self – identify with him – and to destroy him.

In the paradigmatic situation this scenario plays out in the opposite configuration for girls, who identify with their mother while desiring their father as a love object. But normally the drama plays out to some degree in both directions for both girls and boys: all children early in life desire more from both parents, or parent surrogates, than they can give. We want total possession of them. Thus, we lust for both, find each to obstruct our aims with respect to the other, and become jealous of each for the satisfactions he or she can attain that we cannot. As a result we feel both love and hostility toward each and identify with each in our longing for the privileges we envy.

Eventually, in the process that will initiate the formation of a superego, children recognize their desires cannot be met and in the interest of survival repress them, the conflicts surrounding them left unresolved. In abandoning their powerful libidinal strivings for their parents, and in beginning to individuate from the parents as they grow, children experience the loss of them. The loss prompts them to internalize or *introject* their parents as a means of retaining them. That is what people often do after the loss of a love object.

Our first identifications, with the parents, last longest and have the profoundest effect on our character. They form the core of the superego, which assumes the special position the parents held for the child, as an ideal and an authority. In that position it embodies those of the parents' traits the child emulates, including the repressive role the parents played against the child's Oedipal strivings.

In absorbing the repressive function, the superego borrows the parents' strength. But the harshness it comes to display exaggerates the power the parents actually wielded in real life. Freud develops an explanation of this asymmetry later in *The Ego and the Id* and in subsequent works.

Two elements solidify the formation of a superego. One is the existence of a long period of helplessness and dependence in human childhood, which perpetuates the sense of the parents as indispensable and produces the incentive to continue their influence afterward. The other element is the latency period in libidinal development, which is bookended by its flowering in early childhood and its reemergence in adolescence. It comprises the retreat of sexual life during middle-childhood brought about by the repression of the Oedipal complex; the ebbing of sexual interest makes way for the introjection of the parents and the consolidation of the other sequelae of the repression on which the superego draws, like the reaction-formations of morality, shame, and disgust (Freud, 1925b, p. 37).

As children grow older and gradually detach from their parents, the superego incorporates the influence of authorities other than the parents whom the child has encountered in reality. These include teachers and other parties in the growing person's immediate environment, as well as heroes and other public figures whom the individual knows only remotely. When people incorporate these later influences, they no longer introject the person behind the influences, having developed egos that are stronger than their infantile ones were. To these authorities they add, finally, the influence of fate or destiny, which many people find their way to personifying in some manner. Most transfer this final guiding influence to a remote parental figure, or remote parental figures, of some kind, for example Providence, God, or Nature, to whom they envision themselves connected libidinally, as mythologies and folk traditions express.

Freud telegraphs here and expands on later (see Chapter 11 of this book) the scope of the superego's monumental contribution to our social and cultural universe: The superego encompasses the so-called higher nature of humans, including morality, religion, and social feeling. These institutions, as Freud will explain, arise, like the superego as a whole, from the most basic strata of our emotional life – from our Oedipal longings, our repression of those longings, and our internalizing of our parents and the authority they represent.

Thus does Freud offer an alternative to the intuitive and predominant view that morality and religion, indeed all that is expected of our higher nature, arise from a lofty place in the human mind, or from God as the ultimate lofty place. His superego, as the continuation of the longing for the father, contains the seed from which religion evolved: our judgment that we fall short of our ego-ideal makes way for religious humility, to which believers appeal in their longing for the father, recast as a god; likewise, the tensions between the demands of conscience and the actual performance of the ego form the basis of guilt and hence of morality.

The social feelings that emanate from the superego arise from identifications made not with parents but with peers or siblings toward whom we once felt rivalrous for the attentions of the parents or other authorities. The identifications replace hostile impulses we could not realize because of the repercussions they might have provoked, including the breakdown of the group.[2]

After digressing to trace the evolutionary origins of his tripartite schema,[3] Freud concludes his presentation of the superego with a return to the observation from which he staged the presentation: that apparently high mental faculties like criticism and conscience can operate unconsciously, thus showing affinities with both ego and id function and falling squarely under neither. Understood now as emanations of the superego, these faculties draw on the id, which is unconscious, as well as on the ego.

THE LIFE AND DEATH INSTINCTS REVISITED

Freud next attempts to integrate his new structural taxonomy – id, ego, and superego – with his recently revised theory of the instincts, which he now conceives as divided into the life and death instincts

[2]   Freud elaborates the mechanism of peer-identification in his *Group Psychology and the Analysis of the Ego* (1921).

[3]   Freud supposes that both primeval humans and far simpler organisms exhibit the differentiation between an ego and an id. The id contains instinctual endowment and the ego the influence of the external world. In any animal that learns, which is to say any animal that adjusts its behavior in response to its experience, the function Freud calls ego exists. The ego itself, in the light of this function, Freud says, does not inherit anything. It is strictly individual. However, when given experiences have recurred with sufficient strength, in sufficient numbers of individuals and across many generations, he says, they become transformed into experiences of the id. The id's contents can be inherited. When the ego forms its superego, which draws from the id, it may be resurrecting residues of these archaic egos and bringing them into play; Freud takes up this theme in Chapter IV of *Totem and Taboo* (1913b) and in *Group Psychology and the Analysis of the Ego* (1921) and *Moses and Monotheism* (1939). Aside from a remark in his posthumously published *An Outline of Psychoanalysis* (1940a) that a superego must exist wherever a long period of dependency occurs, Freud does not discuss the possibility of a superego in animals.

(see Chapter 8 here). He reminds readers that life embodies both instincts, and both appear, in varying amounts, in "every particle of living substance" (Freud, 1923, p. 41). We may think of the opposition between the two sets of instincts as that between a building up and a breaking down, he says, as expressed by the physiological processes of anabolism and catabolism, respectively.

Critical to Freud's conception and ultimately to the functioning of the agencies of the mind is the way in which the life and death instincts interact within the individual. The interaction begins with the neutralization of the death instincts by the life instincts, introduced in *Beyond the Pleasure Principle*: The organism stays alive, rather than dies, insofar as the life instincts bind, or contain, the death instinct and divert it to the outside.[4]

The origin of aggression

That very diversion of the death instinct to the outside, which occurs "over the musculature," creates aggression, or as Freud labels it at this juncture, an *instinct of destruction* (Freud, 1923, p. 41). He characterizes aggression, thus described, as a case of instinctual *fusion* (Freud, 1923, p. 41): Aggression and its various subtypes, like sadism, are instances of a melding of the life and death instincts,[5] allowing that what can come together in this fashion can also come apart.

The severity of the superego

Insofar as the life and death instincts can fuse, Freud says, they must also be able to *de-fuse* (Freud, 1923, p. 41). De-fusion occurs, he

---

4   In *The Ego and the Id* Freud couches the conception of how the organism manages not to die upon creation in context of the creation specifically of multicellular organisms. Given that multicellular organisms do not expire upon their creation, Freud says, the death instinct present in individual cells must be neutralized by the life instincts present when individual cells come together (Freud, 1923, p. 41). The conjugation represents the life instincts directly, and its timing supports the interplay of the life instincts in sustaining the individual. See Chapter 8, on *Beyond the Pleasure Principle*, for background to this view.

5   Freud will later equivocate about whether there can ever be a culture of pure death instinct, with no admixture of Eros, coming nearly to an affirmative answer and then hedging (see Chapter 11 and Epilogue).

thinks, any time erotic impulses become transformed into other kinds of impulses, by means of sublimation or identification, for instance – as when we sublimate the lust for another into a different striving, such as artistic creation or nonstop work, or when we internalize an object in lieu of pursuing it. When these transformations occur we abandon the aim of sexual gratification for a tamer alternative. With such *desexualization*, erotic impulses, and hence the life instincts, become diminished such that they have less strength to bind, and thus to neutralize, the death instincts. The death instincts, thus liberated, gain in potency.

It is with reference to this process of de-fusion that Freud begins to explain the severity of the superego. As we now know, when people introject their parents, forming what will become the superego, they take into their ego the external objects toward which they had until then directed their libidinal strivings. This leaves the libidinal strivings with no external target. Those strivings, thus redirected toward the ego and tamed by their abandonment of their external aims, lack the strength to bind and deflect the person's death instincts to the degree they did before. The liberated death instincts, left to operate within, inject the repressive side of the superego with additional vigor, thus conferring on it a degree of harshness the original model(s) lacked.

The id and the instincts

The id, in its striving for fulfillment of its sexual aims, expresses the life instincts. But it realizes the death instinct as well insofar as it seeks to discharge the tensions – the impulses – that arise within it, whatever they may be. In the latter trend, it observes the constancy principle, on account of which we seek to lower stimulus as far as possible or at least keep it constant; the constancy principle, on Freud's conception, is a pure expression of the death instinct (see Chapter 8 here). Thus, the id expresses the opposition between the life and death instincts, as opposed to an alloy between them: in that opposition, the life instincts introduce fresh tensions into the system, while the death instincts act to undo the tensions.[6]

THE EGO'S INTERDEPENDENT RELATIONS

In a concluding chapter Freud elaborates further on the peculiar position of the ego within the tripartite division of the mind. Hardly the autonomous unit we might naïvely conceive it to be, it is more a way-station through which we route three powerful influences: the id, representing our instinctual urges, the external reality, and the super-ego, which as a derivative of the unconscious id imposes its own compulsions. The ego in this position serves as both master and much put-upon subject of those three influences, as Freud explains.

As master, the ego imposes on the id as much control as the id will abide, the ego developing from merely obeying instinctual impulses to regulating them. In addition to deploying vicissitudes like repression and sublimation for particularly threatening impulses, it interposes thinking between impulse and action and thereby enables the delay of action and the control of motility. Enriched by its experiences in the outside world, the ego orients the individual there and tests its own processes against reality. It also orders events in time: being connected to consciousness, in which impressions arrive and expire, it can organize its impressions into a series in which one comes before and the next after, and the next after that, and so on (see Chapter 7). Although it does not control the superego, it tries to escape the superego's disparagement and courts its approval.

In its role as subject, the ego struggles to serve the same three forces: the libidinal impulses of the id, external reality, and the harsh superego. As mediator between the id and reality the ego often acquiesces to the headstrong id, because, as derived, it is

---

[6] In additional notes, Freud points out that the most complete realization of the build-up and discharge of tensions is the sexual act, which, he notes, culminates in the release of sexual substances and all tension. Thus the aftermath of copulation retains an affinity with dying. The vicissitude of sublimation, deployed by the ego, meanwhile, aids the id's program of reducing tension insofar as sublimation discharges some, though not all, of the tension of the original impulse it redirects.

constitutionally weaker and, Freud interpolates, it wants to court the id's favor, so the id can love it. It does this by rationalizing the id's demands, construing them as compatible with either reality or the demands of the superego when they conflict. Thus we might steal when we know we shouldn't because, we might rationalize, "the store can always get another one." The ego can also acquiesce, again against its wishes or better judgment, to the bidding of the external world out of fear of loss of love or other threatening repercussions: if asked by a companion to steal, we do so under threat of abandonment. The ego arouses the superego's suspicion at minimal provocation, allowing the superego to unleash its wrath: we ought not to steal, and that we would even contemplate it simply shows us for the no-good, miserable wretch we are and always have been.

The relation between the ego and superego stands out as the most interesting and most complex of the three interdependent relations in which the ego participates – with the id, external world, and superego, respectively. Freud focuses his discussion on it.

The superego looms apart from and over the ego, replacing and sustaining the relationship to the ego children had to their parents. It dominates even the mature ego, which acts at the superego's behest as unconditionally as the child complied with the exhortations of the parents. The relationship between ego and superego becomes skewed in this way because of the conditions of its formation. The ego, Freud says, forms principally from the identifications we make with the people we have loved and gradually detached from, and the superego coalesces from the earliest of these identifications. Those earliest identifications retain their potency throughout our lives both because the ego, when still unformed, had no integrity with which to resist them and because they arise by way of the Oedipal complex and the raging and unresolved emotions it puts into play. We internalize the parents we both loved and feared, whose potential abandonment of us we dreaded above all else, and whom we also despised for their thwarting of our will. Exactly how those raging emotions regroup in the superego is the subject of Freud's subsequent writings (see Chapters 10 and 11 here); for now we can extract that the relation between ego and superego, given its roots in the Oedipal complex, is a fraught one.[7]

Freud believes the severity of the superego manifests in, among other outcomes, guilt and anxiety.

Guilt

The resulting guilt is demonstrated in different ways in a variety of clinical patterns, and also appears in the healthy.

Particularly telling is the *negative therapeutic reaction* (Freud, 1923, p. 49), in which patients cannot abide any praise from the therapist or any hopefulness about their treatment. The usual resistances to recovery – rebelliousness against the therapist, inaccessibility due to narcissism, and gains from illness such as avoidance of the outside world – cannot account for the patients' profound negativism. Analysis suggests that what drives it is a moral factor, a sense of guilt, which Freud says expresses the superego's condemnation of the ego and reflects the tension that dynamic creates.[8] Accordingly, he suspects the severity of the superego underlies all extreme cases of neurosis.

The different kinds of neurosis vary according to the degree to which the ego acquiesces to the superego's judgment and according to whether patients experience the rage of the superego and the resulting guilt consciously. Patients do experience that rage in cases of obsessional neurosis and melancholia, according to Freud.

---

[7]   Freud infers a further contribution of the superego's connection to the Oedipal period to the superego's harshness. He supposes the Oedipal conflict dates to earliest times historically and assumed a particularly violent form at its origin. Remnants of that violence remain in the human psyche, ready to fuel individuals' emotions when Oedipal sentiments are aroused. Freud believes the presumption of phylogenetic influences to be justified on the strength of the mismatch between the emotion we exhibit in our struggles with our first objects and the emotion that would follow from those experiences alone (Freud, 1913b). That early emotion – the ferocity and the anguish – in his estimation, exceeds what day-by-day events would warrant, even in the eyes of a child for whom events take on outsize proportions.

[8]   Freud suggests some of that tension may be vitiated and the negativism weakened as a source of satisfaction if patients manage through transference to replace the superego with the analyst; the guilt may surface in that context such that patient and therapist can work through and disarm it.

A man with obsessional neurosis washes his hands over and over again, for instance, ostensibly on account of his detection of new sources of potential contamination, but really in response to a driving imperative whose origin remains unknown. Because the origin was never recognized and therefore never satisfied, the imperative continues, relentlessly. The battery by that imperative expresses the rage of the superego, which holds the ego accountable for the putative transgression at the imperative's base. Except perhaps through psychoanalysis, the driving transgression and its history cannot be reconstructed. Did the sufferer actually do something bad? Indeed do so but only in his child's mind's eye? Internalize and so assume guilt for a failing on the part of a parent? The ego, in a case of obsessional neurosis, accepts that guilt insofar as the individual complies with the manifest imperative – in our example, by washing his hands. But it repudiates the charge insofar as the sufferer experiences only an urgency to wash his hands and does not know any wider guilt.

Melancholics, meanwhile, assailed consciously by the superego in their sense of despair, also feel great guilt in connection with circumstances both known and unknown. Freud ascribes the difference between obsessional neurosis and melancholia to whether the target of the objectionable impulses is lodged outside or inside the patient's ego. In obsessional neurosis the object of the impulses the superego abhors exists outside the ego: the simultaneously loved and deplored parents, whose abandonment the hand-washer once feared on account of his engaging in what he internalized as dirty acts, still exist as objects external to his own self. In melancholia, on the other hand, the ego has internalized the object of the superego's wrath through identification: a depressive feels herself to be a wretched human being, when it is really others, whom she has introjected, at whom she would like to level that accusation (see Freud, 1917c).

Melancholics, Freud adds, run the risk of suicide – the complete destruction of the ego. Obsessive neurotics, by contrast, having situated their objects outside their ego, have a source against which to direct their aggression, as well as their love.

Whereas the guilt inflicted by the superego remains conscious in one form or another in obsessional neurosis and melancholia, it is repressed by the ego and hence remains unconscious in hysterics like Anna O. She, unlike an obsessive neurotic, felt no imperative to do something to stave off danger; she simply became unable to drink. Unlike a melancholic, she did not feel herself a miserable, valueless wretch.

Reflecting on the nature of the guilt healthy people harbor, Freud surmises a large portion of it remains unconscious, much as it does in hysterics but according to a different logic. Guilt arises on the basis of our conscience. Our conscience is launched when we repress our Oedipal strivings, abandon and internalize the object we once pursued (say, a parent), and replace it with a new taskmaster, the superego. We now harbor, in place of the real or imagined injunctions and judgments we perceived our parents to deliver, an internal arbiter of our thoughts and actions, the arbiter exaggerated in its ferocity on account of the Oedipal dynamic. Conscience and the guilt it may provoke are the voice of that arbiter. Because the Oedipal complex, once repressed, is unconscious, so are the immediate sequelae of the repression, like the superego, conscience, and guilt. Conscience and guilt may operate consciously as well, when we reflect on and evaluate impulses and actions of which we are fully aware.

Freud notes in passing the possibility that an unconscious sense of guilt of the sort that operates in the neuroses he has described can turn people into criminals. To satisfy the need for punishment the ego feels at the hands of the superego, they commit acts for which they will indeed be punished. Freud reports evidence the guilt existed before the crime, making the guilt likely to have motivated the crime rather than to have resulted from it. The crime brings relief to the perpetrator who can now attach the guilt to something real and immediate (Freud, 1923, p. 52, also Freud, 1916, Section III).

Freud observes, in conformity with this analysis, that the more people check their aggressiveness toward the external world, the more severe, which is to say the more aggressive, their superego becomes and the more they become filled with guilt and doubt about their moral fealty. Freud ventures that here, as in melancholia, a withheld destructive instinct comes back at the self in the form of criticism and harshness of the superego. The causation does not run the other way, however, he insists: it is not the case that the severe superego comes into being first and prompts the withholding of aggressiveness. Without some dynamic of the sort Freud outlines – a withholding of aggression on account of some other imperative – it would be difficult to explain the particular severity of the superego (see Chapter 10 under "Aggression and masochism" for further elaboration).

On further consideration, Freud notes, even ordinary morality exhorts the individual with a harshly restraining voice, as expressed by the command "Thou *shalt*...." Freud speculates that the dynamic that represses the Oedipal complex and replaces it with the obscure superego may contribute something else – the conception of a higher entity that relentlessly and unforgivingly metes out punishment (Freud, 1923, pp. 54–55).

Anxiety

The ego, threatened as it is by dangers from the three masters that prey upon it – in addition to the superego, the id and the external world – becomes the seat of anxiety. Although Freud surmises the ego fears from the id and the external world the threat of being overwhelmed or annihilated, he cannot as of this writing identify precisely what it is the ego fears from either source.[9] He is able to point with greater certainty to the nature of the anxiety that arises in connection with the superego: the dread of conscience, or the idea that we have done something badly wrong, on account of which the threat of abandonment looms.[10] But

---

[9]   Freud develops his views on anxiety significantly in his later (1926) *Inhibitions, Symptoms, and Anxiety*, where, among other additions, he traces the sense of overwhelm and the fear of annihilation to the experience of birth. He suggests the physical concomitants of the later experience of anxiety retain some of the trappings of our response to birth, e.g., the vigorous attempt to inflate the lungs to avoid suffocation.

[10]   In *The Ego and the Id*, Freud depicts the content of the threat of abandonment, or separation, as a fear of castration. Three years later, in *Inhibitions, Symptoms, and*

now it is the superego's, as opposed to the parents,' abandonment we fear, the superego having replaced the parents as our most immediate source of love and protection.

Freud concludes with an aside on the fear of death, a species of anxiety he believes is illuminated by his introduction of the superego. He begins by rejecting the popular idea that anxiety itself consists of a fear of death. Because we have never experienced death, it cannot be what we fear. In fearing death we must be fearing something we have experienced, for example the threat of abandonment, or separation, but now thorough and final. The dread pertains more exactly to the ego's part in the separation. Dying, or the expectation of dying, Freud says, involves a major relinquishment of narcissistic libido: it consists of our giving up our selves. The fear of death, Freud speculates following out this line of thought, could consist of the ego's giving up itself, casting itself off from the protecting force of the superego. Freud envisions the unfolding of the dynamic in two different instances, one in which the fear of death arises as an internal process of the kind that occurs in melancholia, and the other as a reaction to an external danger.

The fear of death in melancholia has the greater transparency. In that condition the ego gives itself up as a result of feeling abandoned and hated by the superego. The ego wants to feel loved. Life to it, therefore, has the same meaning as being loved, specifically by the superego; the superego in this role represents the id, which establishes the objects of the libido. Once the superego has developed it serves the role the parents served earlier. Many people, as noted earlier, later project that role into Providence or Destiny, or God.

When, on the other hand, the ego faces extreme external danger, meaning a threat it cannot overcome by its own strength, it will draw the same conclusion as it does in melancholia: all protecting forces have abandoned it. In the face of that eventuality, it gives up; it abandons its will to live and lets itself die. The prototype for this

Anxiety (1926), he broadens the content to include fears accessible to both genders, like separation from our loving others.

emotional circumstance lies in the anxiety provoked by birth and by the anxiety babies subsequently experience in longing for their first protector, the mother, when separated from her. The fear of death traces ultimately to the same source, the anxiety provoked by separation from the protector.

10 Pleasure revised: "An economic problem in masochism" (1924)

> If mental processes are governed by the pleasure principle in such a way
> that their first aim is the avoidance of unpleasure and the obtaining of
> pleasure, masochism is incomprehensible.

– S. Freud, "The economic problem of masochism," 1924, p.159

*In this brief but important piece Freud makes explicit a change in his
conception of pleasure, a change consistent with his recognition,
alluded to in* Beyond the Pleasure Principle *(see Chapter 8 here),
that pleasure may arise from an increase, as well as from a decrease,
in stimulus. He formalizes his addition of the nirvana principle to the
pleasure and reality principles as the basis of our motivation. He goes
on to use the dichotomy of the life and death instincts to articulate
and explain the differences among them. The springboard for the
revision of the theory is Freud's observation of the phenomenon of
masochism, which contradicts the pleasure principle as he originally
construed it.*

THE PROBLEM

The existence of masochism as a human practice raises the question of how, assuming the pleasure principle operates, people can
knowingly inflict pain on themselves. After all, the pleasure principle holds that we seek first and foremost to avoid pain and
where possible to cultivate pleasure. But Freud avers that masochism does not in fact violate the pleasure principle, because we
may sometimes find pleasure even in pain. That we may do so,
however, presupposes a conception of pleasure that can accommodate pain.

PLEASURE

Until this point Freud has coupled the pleasure principle with the constancy principle derived from Gustav Fechner.[1] According to the constancy principle, which Freud now calls the nirvana principle to signify the perfection of stasis,[2] organisms strive to keep their level of excitation as low as possible or at least constant. It is because the state of death perfectly realizes the elimination of all excitation, or tension, that Freud originally allied the pleasure principle with death instincts.

But he now adds that pleasures exist that correspond to an increase in tension, the pleasure of sexual foreplay a clear example, and unpleasures that arise from the diminution of tension – boredom perhaps. It follows that pleasure and unpleasure must engage a qualitative factor as well as a quantitative one; that factor, although as yet largely unknown, might be connected with the rhythm of increases and decreases of stimulus, as opposed to only the direction of their changes. This prospect is developed further in *Civilization and its Discontents* (see Chapter 11 here).

Freud extrapolates an historical narrative from these reflections on the affiliation between the death instinct and stimulus reduction, and the apparent variability of sources of pleasure. He supposes the nirvana principle, linked with the instinct toward death as the utter absence of tension, arose before the pleasure principle and underwent a modification to produce it. The modification, Freud imagines, developed from the intervention of the life instincts, or the libido, which introduce tension into the system; by extension, pleasure that results from an increase in tension requires the intervention of the life instincts.

Thus, whereas the nirvana or constancy principle remains the affiliate of the death instinct, pleasure now represents the demands of the life instincts. The reality principle, which in turn modifies the pleasure principle, expresses the influence of the outside world. All three principles coexist within the individual, though they may

[1]   See Chapter 8, Note 14.   [2]   After Low, 1920.

occasionally conflict, as, for example, when we check our impulse to jump off the garage roof on recognizing that the concrete below won't absorb our landing too well – representing the clash between the pleasure and reality principles; or, our wish for peace and silence one evening (nirvana) competes with our desire to attend a friend's party.

This revision in the conception of pleasure allows masochism to be consistent with the pleasure principle. Given that pleasure can arise through an increase in stimuli, it follows that masochism, as an instance of such increase in its cultivation of pain, can bring pleasure.

VARIETIES OF MASOCHISM

Freud identifies three kinds of masochism – erotogenic, feminine, and moral – each inclining us to experience a different kind of pleasure in pain.

Erotogenic masochism, the lust for pain, underlies the other two varieties and has roots in the biological constitution of the individual. It derives from the capability of any intense process within the organism to excite the sexual instinct, which in turn derives from an infantile physiological mechanism, Freud says (1924, p. 417). But that mechanism alone, rooted as it is in the individual's own sensations, won't explain sadism, or the infliction of pain on another, which is presumably a "vicissitude" of masochism (see Chapter 5 here). Freud fills the explanatory gap with the dynamic he elaborated earlier wherein the life instincts bind and deflect the death instinct that would otherwise destroy the organism (1920, 1923; see Chapters 8 and 9 here). But not all of the death instinct gets deflected, he now hypothesizes. A portion remains within, where, as he specified before, it becomes bound by the life instincts operating there. The result of that intermingling – of the portion of the death instinct that has remained internal, and the life instincts – allows the sexually arousing experience of pain that defines erotogenic masochism. This is "primary masochism," a proclivity present at the outset of life and not derived from any other trend, unlike masochism as depicted in

"Instincts and their vicissitudes" (1915a), where it is derived from sadism (see Chapter 5 here).[3]

Feminine masochism lies at the base of masochistic perversion, a variety of masochism of which males are capable, contrary to the likely assumption that the condition applies to females. Individuals displaying that trend wish to be beaten, bound, defiled, degraded, and even mutilated and thereby forced into unconditional obedience. They want to be treated as a naughty child, and specifically at the hands of the father, the desire deriving from the wish to assume the passive position in coitus with him. In erotogenic masochism as well, the condition links with a fantasy of the administration of the pain by a loved one. In both cases the fantasy links more deeply with the wish to assume the passive, or traditionally feminine, role in coitus, according to Freud's surmise based on the analysis of cases.

Moral masochism differs from the other two forms in that it has no clear sexual overtones and no fantasized tormentor. The individual desires only punishment, regardless of the source. True moral masochists, Freud says, turn their cheek at any chance to receive a blow. Although such destructiveness absent sexual overtones might seem to make this form of masochism an expression of pure death instinct, Freud believes the attribution would prove too narrow an account. Given that the two more perspicuous forms of masochism have an identifiable sexual component, thereby implicating the life instincts, Freud wonders whether moral masochism might not do the same, even if less obviously. He concludes it does, after a close analysis that both draws on and elaborates his account of the superego.

Freud begins the analysis with a return to the negative therapeutic reaction, which presents an extreme and thus unmistakable example of moral masochism. In *The Ego and the Id* (1923; see Chapter 9 here), Freud attributed the reaction to the oppression of the ego by a particularly severe superego, so severe the patient needs

[3] Even in this later view, "secondary masochism" can arise, building on the primary form, when sadism, now a vicissitude of primary masochism, encounters obstacles in its outward trajectory and turns back on the self. See under *Moral masochism*, next.

to suffer to assuage a sense of guilt. The ego reacts with anxiety to its perception that it has failed to meet the demands of the superego, and the anxiety spurs the generation of the reaction.

Implicit in this and other cases of moral masochism, Freud now adds, are two sides to the ego–superego relationship. On the one hand, the superego has the impulse to punish the ego insofar as the ego does not match up to the superego's expectations: it lashes out against the ego with heightened sadism, and the browbeaten ego submits to the sadism. An expression of that side of the relationship appears in the extreme moral inhibition and particularly sensitive conscience moral masochists exhibit. On the other side, and it is this that constitutes moral masochism proper, the ego seeks punishment. In the typical condition the superego's cruelty reaches consciousness, in the form of severe restraint, whereas the ego's desire for punishment – its masochism – eludes awareness and must be inferred from sufferers' behavior.

Freud is now able to connect this purely psychological form of masochism with the two other and more obvious types. Once the unconscious sense of guilt is understood as a need for punishment, it shows a ready affinity with the feminine, or passive, form of masochism, and, like the latter, shows its Oedipal roots – to be beaten by the father or taken as his sexual object – or rather a reanimation of them. It thus retains the sexual element connoted by the term "masochism."

Although the desire for punishment may lead to an apparently heightened morality, it may also invite wrongdoing so as to elicit the wanted punishment. In that sense it may prompt people to act against their own interest, so as, again, to bring about the ill fortune they believe they deserve.

Both the severity of the superego against the ego and the ego's search for punishment – its masochism – may receive impetus from still another source. In one of the natural "vicissitudes" that arise with instincts (see Chapter 5 here), when we find ourselves unable to deliver the full brunt of our destructive urges against others, we turn them around on our self; there they escape external detection and its repercussions. The superego continues the deflected destructiveness as a lashing out, now against the ego rather than against the other, and the ego willingly absorbs it.

AGGRESSION AND MASOCHISM

More broadly, Freud says, when we inhibit aggression, it may come back against ourselves, in the form of a punishing conscience, or superego, as well as in the form of an ego seeking punishment. That dynamic illustrates the counterintuitive circumstance that the suppression of an instinct can produce guilt; intuitively we would expect the realization of an instinct – the commission, rather than omission, of the deed – to arouse guilt in us. For, Freud reasons, guilt is none other than the ego's acquiescence to the superego's accusations of impropriety. The accusations, in turn, represent aggression against the ego. But we now know the superego can aggress against the ego when the ego has inhibited outward-directed aggression, as well as when it commits or contemplates an unworthy act. The former case is the deflection just mentioned, in which, in fear of repercussions from the outside, we deflect our aggression back against ourselves where it can discharge more safely.

Thus does the superego assail the ego all the more when the ego holds back, rather than delivers, an aggressive impulse aimed at an external other. And so, the more we inhibit aggression against others, the more punitive and sensitive our conscience becomes; the heightened conscience is the curtailed aggression redirected against the self. It is that heightened sensibility, originating in the renunciation of impulse, that will inhibit the realization of future such impulses.

In this way a further counterintuitive view arises, that the renunciation of instinctual urges preceded the ethical requirement that we renounce them. First, we inhibited our aggression under the threat of external repercussions. Next, instead of provoking condemnation from the outside, we incurred the wrath of the superego. Then, the superego delivered the condemnation we had expected from the outside, which is now fueled by the unused aggressive energy.

We might more naturally imagine the reverse scenario, that the ethical requirement came first and brought about the renunciation of instinct. But, Freud points out, that order of events would leave the ethical requirement unexplained. What, he asks, would be the source of the energetic imperative that we must not – let us say – aggress?

Similarly, intuition would suggest that the more people abstain from aggressing, the less their egos would require suspicious oversight, because they would be inhibiting the actions that could get them into trouble. But it is precisely in such individuals that condemnatory reprimands reach their highest pitch, the expression of inhibited aggression having found a willing target.

Freud sees in moral masochism a premier case of instinctual *fusion* (see Chapter 9), of the perfect melding of the death and life, or death and specifically sexual, instincts. It engages both the aforementioned portion of the death instinct left inside when the remainder was forced outward as aggression, and the portion of the remainder that was turned back against the subject. It blends with these the erotic components aroused by pain and by the object from which the individual withdrew the aggression, as well as the individual's endogenous life instincts.

Moral masochism poses a danger, Freud says, because it gives expression to the portion of the death instinct that remained internal to the organism instead of being turned outward; that portion, now realized, can operate destructively on the self. However, on account of the eroticism present in all varieties of masochism, even our own self-destruction would occur with a modicum of libidinal excitation.

II Civilization, morality, and the pursuit of pleasure: *Civilization and its Discontents* (1930)

> We can at last grasp two things perfectly clearly: the part played by love in the origin of conscience and the fatal inevitability of the sense of guilt.
>
> – S. Freud, *Civilization and its Discontents*, p. 132

Freud's seminal Civilization and its Discontents *brings still further elaboration on the oppressive internal forces he calls the superego. Those forces occasion the malaise all humans are destined to feel on account of the critical role the forces play in fostering civilized life. Their necessity derives from the unflinching dominance of the pleasure principle in our individual mental lives and the instincts upon which the pleasure principle plays.* Civilization and its Discontents *delivers the final refinement of these various elements of Freud's system and a crowning integration of them. En route, it takes us on a wide-ranging tour through the psyche and the history of civilization, as Freud understands them.*

Freud begins the narrative proper with a documentation of the ubiquity of the human striving for happiness, which persists despite the fact that we seldom achieve it and mostly aim, also with limited success, to avoid pain; this is the program of the pleasure principle. Surmising that human relations are responsible for our suffering, he counts among the difficulties that civilization, which we rightly cherish nonetheless, requires that we restrict our possibilities for satisfaction. We have to renounce or at least redirect our instincts, and to deprive an instinct of satisfaction must occur at a great cost.

Having now identified civilization as both prize and culprit Freud asks how it arose and how it came to compromise our happiness to the degree it does. He offers that it was founded in "love and necessity," which manifest, respectively, in the pull toward family and our pursuit of our material wellbeing, the latter enhanced by community efforts like work in common. However, given the strength with which family ties pull people away from the wider community, common interest will not hold that community together. As a result we have come to be bound also by "libidinal ties" outside the family, as the precept to "love thy neighbor as thyself" exhorts.

But the precept arouses Freud's suspicion. Our neighbors are at least as likely to abuse us as to love us in return. And so our loving them unconditionally doesn't make sense on the face of it.

Why, then, must we do so? We must do so, Freud eventually concludes, to check human aggression, the idea being that if we love one another, we are less likely to destroy, i.e., aggress against, one another. Aggression, he now decides, and not the tension between intimate and communal life, poses the main threat to civilization. Reiterating the derivation of aggression from the death instinct, Freud reconceives civilization as the struggle between the life instincts, or Eros, and Death, or Thanatos, the two forces that under-gird the individual human life.

Civilization has a more far-reaching way to inhibit human aggressiveness, namely the institution of individual guilt. The check-ing of our aggression at every turn, in our development and through our lives, results in the deflection of aggression inward, where it manifests in the outsized severity of the superego. We experience the lashings, insofar as we acquiesce to them, as guilt, a guilt that may be rising to intolerable levels. It is because of this, our own individual embodiment of the requirements of civilization, that we are unhappy in it.

THE PURSUIT OF HAPPINESS

Asking what we show by our behavior the purpose of our lives to be, Freud suggests we all seek happiness. The pursuit of happiness expresses the program of the pleasure principle, which impels us toward the removal of pain and the cultivation of pleasure. However, that program cannot possibly succeed given both our constitution and the way the world works. Happiness in the narrowest sense, Freud says, arises from the sudden satisfaction of needs dammed up to a high degree, as embodied by sexual love. Satisfaction of this kind necessarily arises only episodically. Any desirable situation that is prolonged produces at most mild contentment. Meanwhile, we suffer easily, from our bodies, the external world, and our relations with other people.

In the light of these limitations to our prospects for happiness, we moderate our claims to it and mainly try not to suffer too much. We have evolved numerous means for mitigating our suffering. These include: withdrawal from the world; the chemical alteration of our organism, for example through alcohol; the subduing of our instincts, for example through Yoga; sublimation, which involves a shifting of our instinctual aims from their original intent; illusion such as that afforded by art and the enjoyment of beauty. Some of these methods for mitigating suffering, for example the engagement with art or the enjoyment of beauty, produce at most a mild narcosis, as Freud describes it, a transient withdrawal from our needs; yet we would be loath to do without them.[1] We might add religion to this list, in its promise of redemption, salvation, and protection, and its sense of community; Freud will have more to say about that promise momentarily.

Although the program of becoming happy cannot find fulfillment, Freud observes, we will not give it up. In our continued pursuit of it we do well to follow diverse paths, because any single path may fail; for instance, we may lose the object of our love.

---

[1]   Freud provides interesting passing commentary on the nature of our love of beauty (anticipated in his *Three Essays on Sexuality* (1905a, p. 156 n2 and p. 209)). The comments merit attention because they address the quality of feeling beauty arouses, as opposed to the conditions that appear to elicit the feeling; most commentary on the subject addresses the latter. Beauty, Freud says, has a mildly intoxicating quality whose origin eludes discernment. He wonders whether the reaction might not trace ultimately to the field of sexual feeling. Historically, he speculates, beauty might have evolved as a property attaching to secondary sexual characteristics, such as the face or the figure, those designed to attract, as opposed to those evolved to serve the act. See the Epilogue, here, for further discussion.

Religion restricts the choice of pathways. One must subscribe, unquestioningly, to a set of beliefs, in the wake of whose undermining the whole system and the solace it brings will collapse. In thus restricting our choices, religion may spare us the individual neurosis that can result when the world frustrates our needs and desires. But it does so at the expense of our succumbing to a group delusion, a position Freud lays out in his *The Future of an Illusion* (1927a) and summarizes in a preamble to *Civilization and its discontents* (1930): Religion, lacking any basis in fact and imposing an infantilism on its supplicants, mimics the child's longing for the parents and probably traces to it, arising as it does as a palliative for a life that is too hard, painful, and disappointing. Therefore, he concludes, religion belongs in the category of delusion in the roster of different means of alleviating human suffering.

CIVILIZATION AND ITS DEMANDS ON THE PSYCHE

Although we readily accept both our bodies and external, unconquerable nature as sources of our suffering, we are less likely to admit the institution of civilization – our decision to live in groups – to this list.[2] Yet, Freud suspects, the very civilization we cherish may indeed add to our unhappiness. We may be so constructed that civilization, despite our admiration of it, places a burden on us that makes our suffering inevitable.[3] Addressing what it is in civilization that may so compromise us, Freud turns to what civilization is, followed by an initial appraisal of its psychical costs.

Civilization, he says, encompasses the totality of achievements and regulations that distinguish the lives of humans from those of

---

[2]   Most people would easily add to the list of sources of unhappiness society's failures – its inequities, abuses of power, and any other form of oppression it promotes. We are less likely to perceive the mere fact of living in groups and the most basic requirements of doing so in this light.

[3]   Freud warns us, however, not to suppose that earlier civilizations enjoyed any greater happiness than we do. We cannot, from our vantage point, realize the psychical reality of earlier eras and thus cannot judge them.

animals. Those achievements and regulations serve mainly to protect us against nature and manage our relations with one another.

The achievements encompass tool use, or more generally the attempt to make the earth serviceable to people, including the control over fire; also beauty, cleanliness, and order, desiderata that serve little or no practical purpose but on whose presence we insist; and intellectual, scientific, and artistic pursuit, as well as, according to the conventional wisdom, religion and philosophy. The last attainments are held to represent manifestations of our higher mental faculties and the pinnacle of civilization. Closely connected with them is the body of ideas Freud calls our ideals – the notion, for instance, of a possible perfection of individuals, entire peoples, or the whole of humanity.

As for the regulations, the stipulations that manage human relations, civilization can exist only when a majority of a community acts together such that its will proves stronger than the will of any individual. Justice came about to ensure that laws once made would not be broken in favor of any single individual or, ultimately, any individual group. Thus the development of civilization would necessarily have regulated individual freedom, specifically restricting the satisfaction of our instinctual demands.

Civilization is a process, Freud elaborates, comparable to the development of each individual. It brings about changes in our instinctual dispositions so we may continue to satisfy our individual needs while sustaining our life in groups; the satisfaction of our instincts, Freud reminds us, is the "economic task of our lives"(Freud, 1930, p. 96). He notes three mechanisms of change in our instinctual dispositions.

First, some instinctual impulses become fixed into *character traits*, such as parsimony and the emphasis on order and cleanliness. Freud suspects, based on the exaggeration of these traits in neurotic patients, the traits express displaced anal eroticism.[4] The redirection

---

[4]   Anal eroticism is a normal phase of development people ordinarily surmount (see Chapter 1). The overcoming of neurotic fixations, however, requires intervention, typically therapy.

of those instinctual impulses necessarily blocks their achievement of full satisfaction. Given that blocked impulses continue to strive for satisfaction, the traits noted – parsimony, order, and cleanliness – may arise as the result of that striving. In thus answering an internal imperative, the traits might persist even when they exceed material usefulness, as Freud observes they do.

Civilization engineers the alteration of the instincts in a second way through the process of *sublimation*. That mechanism changes the aim of an instinct such that the instinct discharges safely, this time in an alternative pursuit, as opposed to in a fixed response like a character trait. The higher achievements of civilization, and of the individual mind, such as artistic and scientific pursuit and the building of ideology, resulted, and result, from this process, according to Freud.

The third and most profound mechanism of change civilization engenders to preserve itself is a pervasive *renunciation of instinct*, which is to say outright denial of satisfaction. Even the first two mechanisms of the civilizing process, the formation of character traits and sublimation, entail a renunciation of the affected instincts' original aim. But we would not naturally deny our instincts satisfaction. That denial must come at a cost and significantly compromise mental life.

It is on account of the renunciation of instinct that people become hostile to civilization, and the hostility itself exacts a toll on them, as Freud progressively illustrates in the remainder of his book.

THE ORIGINS AND DEVELOPMENT OF CIVILIZATION

Freud proceeds to imagine how civilization might have begun and the factors that might have influenced its subsequent course. He supposes it to have been founded on love, on the one hand, and necessity, on the other. Love produced the family, which formed when individuals wanted to assure genital satisfaction on an ongoing basis and protection for their young.[5] Necessity heightened the sensitivity to the advantages of work in common. Once primal humans discovered

---

5   The same arrangement would also assure perpetuation of the species; however, Freud is
     addressing only the immediate individual motivation to cohabit.

they could improve their circumstances through work, they perceived the further benefit of the combined efforts of a multitude. The multitude could accomplish what any individual could not do alone.

Freud, following other writers of his time, stipulates the hypothetical existence of primal families – hordes – each led by an all-powerful father who ruled with an unrestricted will.[6] Communal life beyond the family began, Freud suggests, when bands of brothers in the primal family came together to dispatch the terrible father. Eventually the sons' antipathy toward the father for his cruelty and greed (the latter, for example, with respect to the available females) exceeded the love they felt for him and their desire for protection by him. They rose up and killed him, discovering they had the best chance of accomplishing the feat by cooperating with one another. Then, recognizing the need to avoid having yet another leader ascend by might, the sons banded together in a more permanent way. They did this by imposing restrictions on themselves; those restrictions resulted eventually in taboo observances that established the first laws.

But the wider community – civilization – would not hold together, Freud realizes, given the incentives of love and necessity alone.

Love, for its part, although the fundament of civilization, soon comes into conflict with it. The family unit, which is created and sustained by love, does not want to lose its individual members to the wider community[7]– yet it has had to do just that as a matter of course in the interest of civilization. Severe restrictions imposed on sexual life also evidence conflict between love and civilization. Civilization for most of its existence has limited love to a single permanent bond and curtailed acceptable sexual choices and activity; all these limitations – frustrations of sexual life, Freud calls them – have

[6] Freud (1913b) cites Darwin (1871) and sources there, acknowledging the speculative nature of the conjecture.

[7] Women, as representatives of the family, Freud says, perpetuate this conflict; Freud's earlier "'Civilized' sexual morality and modern nervous illness" (1908b) provides useful context for this assertion.

compromised our prospects for happiness, as his abundant experience with neurotic patients attests.

As for necessity, common interest does not suffice to hold members of a community together, as in-fighting shows for example. Work, in turn, although ideally suited to unifying people, given both its usefulness and its enhancement by collaboration, does not incite community, because most people disparage, rather than embrace, it (Freud, 1930, p. 80 n1, also p. 75).

THE DOCTRINE OF UNIVERSAL LOVE AND THE INCLINATION TO AGGRESSION

Civilization might have counteracted those factors by developing into a collection of couples, each individual bound to the other libidinally and each unit joined to the wider community by work and interests in common. But it did not develop that way. Instead it insisted on the extension of libidinal bonds to the wider community, including strangers. In that extension, libidinal interest – love – assumes an *aim-inhibited* form, like friendship, according to Freud, sensual love being reserved for our intimates; in aim-inhibited love people strive to be near and to further the interests of their others, whereas sensual love aims implicitly or explicitly toward copulation and reproduction.[8] Why, Freud asks, does civilization require this extra bond among people in the entire community?

He finds the solemn and unquestioned ideal of universal love suspect. When we love indiscriminately, we devalue the love we feel for our own people. And why should we love our neighbor as

---

[8] In both forms, love binds people together and exerts a stronger force toward that end than does work or other interests in common. In the case of sensual love, some of that strength comes from the imperative nature of full sexual drive. Freud thinks aim-inhibited love, despite its different end, draws on the same source. Aim-inhibited love, he ventures, originated as fully sensual love and remains as such in people's unconscious. The two overlap in feeling and in function – the function being the binding together of people – which suggests a common origin. Sensual love is the older of the two in its link to reproduction and so may have formed the base from which aim-inhibited love developed, the connection retained in our unconscious as historical forms are. That does not mean that it is in any way sensual love or that it is sensual love we really want when we feel (nonsensual) affection for another.

ourselves? A neighbor who shows us no consideration or goes so far as to hurt or exploit us might even deserve our enmity.

Freud detects in the ideal of universal love a possible reaction-formation – the defense whereby we compensate for unwanted impulses with exaggerated expressions of their opposite, as in the gushing solicitude of the wife who in fact loathes her husband. Aggressive urges, thoroughly inconsistent with universal love, lie within every human. It is those internal urges, in addition to the built-in conflict between individual and community, that threaten to erode our relations with our neighbors.

People are incited to bond with one another to neutralize the aggressive impulses that would otherwise destroy society. Sometimes they do so, not by developing a relationship, but by assimilating the traits of another, in a manifestation of the process Freud calls *identi-fication*. However, the incitement to bond has accomplished little toward fulfilling the injunction to universal love: Humans cannot easily give up aggression.[9]

Insofar as civilization requires the curtailment of the sexual and aggressive urges humans natively harbor, people find it difficult to remain happy in civilization.[10]

[9] In an interesting digression Freud questions the psychological plausibility of the communistic system in its assumption of human good will. At the time Freud wrote, communism was seeing its first trial, in the Soviet Union. The system supposes that people are inherently good and are corrupted by property. Wealth brings power, the assumption goes, and, with power, the temptation to ill-treat our neighbor. Conversely, those from the deprived classes feel inclined to rebel. Were everyone's needs met, people would have no reason to regard others as their enemy. But, Freud says, in abolishing private property, the program would deprive the human love of aggression of one of its primary instruments. The urge would soon find vehicles, for example sex. Private property did not create aggression, which reigned unrestrictedly before property came about and, in individual development, rules the nursery before the end of the anal period. Later in the book he makes passing remarks about possible benefits of the elimination of private property (Freud, 1930, p. 143; Note 20, this chapter).

[10] The prospect for happiness is further undermined by what Freud calls the psychological poverty of groups, referring to the decline in autonomy and intelligence that comes with mob mentality; he envisions that mentality would be elicited by the incitement to bonding among people who would otherwise aggress against one another. (Freud discusses group psychology at length in *Group Psychology and the Analysis of the Ego* (1921)). Freud worries we may find our entire intellectual level in decline and with it our prospects for real satisfaction.

AGGRESSION AND THE THEORY OF INSTINCTS

Having singled out aggression as a central problem for civilization, Freud revisits the position of aggression within his theory of instincts. The original theory distinguished only "hunger," or the ego instincts, and "love," or the sexual instincts, and it accommodated sadism, the force closest to aggression Freud discussed at the time. Sadism fell within both the sexual and ego instincts, he held, in the light of, respectively, the excitement brought about by the production of pain in the object and the drive to master and dominate the object.

With the discovery of narcissism, or the investment of sexual energy, or libido, in the self, the ego and sexual instincts came to seem less distinct. Freud now recognized the possibility that mental life might issue from a single pool of instinctual energy, encompassing both trends, instead of from two pools. But he remained convinced some global differentiation must exist among instincts, some distinction more prominent and more overarching than the now somewhat blurred one he maintained still existed between the sexual and ego instincts.

He saw grounds for the latter continued division in the conflict between the two types of instinct in cases of neurosis: the sexual instincts fuel urges – for example lusts – to which the ego instincts, in their protective function, undertake to deny expression (see Chapters 5 and 8 here). He ultimately found grounds for a more global differentiation in his discovery of the repetition compulsion, described in *Beyond the Pleasure Principle* (1920) (see Chapter 8 here).

The compulsion to repeat even wholly unredeeming experiences prompted Freud to recognize the repetitive quality of all instincts. Each restores an earlier state: the intake of nutrition restores the organism to previous satiety; satisfaction of a sexual impulse restores the previous state of quiescence. He thus inferred the conservative nature of instincts.

Having identified that characteristic of instincts, he wondered whether life in general might not be attempting in some way to return to an initial state, and so sought to identify that state. He distinguished inorganicity as the earliest state of matter on earth, life having arisen later. But everything that lives eventually dies. In doing so it can be seen as returning to that original inorganic state.

Accordingly, Freud posited a death instinct in keeping with which living organisms, in dying, return to the condition from which all life began. The instinct, he further determined, manifests not only at life's end, but throughout life in the reduction of stimulus toward which we strive in the satisfaction of any urge.[11]

The death instinct, or *Thanatos*, is juxtaposed throughout life with the life instincts, or *Eros*, which subsume those instincts Freud originally categorized as sexual or ego instincts. The life instincts add stimulus to the system and drive it toward new and ever greater combinations. Life, Freud emphasizes, consists of the simultaneous and sometimes mutually opposing, operation of both the life and death instincts. The life instincts aim toward the preservation and indefinite recombination of living substance, while the death instinct presses toward its decomposition.

Within this new framework, aggression would seem to fit naturally within the compass of the death instinct, given its end in destruction. Until this work, Freud had derived it from the death instinct, but not ascribed it solely to that force, reasoning as follows: were the death instinct we are born with to operate unimpeded, we would simply expire. But on account of the life instincts that also operate within, a portion of the death instinct is deflected outward in the form of aggression; thus we destroy something instead of simply expiring.

The life instincts, moreover, are involved in activities that count as aggression, as attested to by the fact that sadism and masochism, both forms of aggression, include clear erotic components. These entailments of the life instincts in aggression, Freud recognizes, might seem to weaken the case for affiliating aggression

---

[11]   As per the constancy or nirvana principle Freud distinguished (see Chapter 8).

primarily with the death instinct and to question the prominence of the death instinct generally. But nonerotic aggression, an increasing presence over the course of the early twentieth century, when Freud was writing, attests again to the play of the death instinct. Yet, he notes, even in cases of aggression at its blindest and most destructive, with no erotic aim or payoff, aggressing brings its perpetrators the narcissistic enjoyment of satisfying their old wishes for omnipotence. Thus even it manifests the involvement of the life instincts, given that narcissistic satisfaction embodies both sexual and egoistic trends.

In the end, aggression, although not exclusively a product of the death instinct, invariably expresses and thereby attests to the existence of the two classes of instinct. As destructive, it always engages the death instinct. When manifesting as sadism or masochism, it is sexually tinged and thereby a manifestation also of the life instincts. Even when devoid of any obvious erotic aim and presenting with the evident aim only of destruction, it fulfills our narcissistic desires, thus again implicating the sexual, and hence the life, instincts.

Nonetheless, Freud believes it reasonable to assume henceforth, on the basis of the existence and ubiquity of nonerotic forms of aggression, an original, free-standing inclination in humans toward aggression. The inclination is, however, always alloyed in some proportion with the life instincts.

Freud now revises his definition of civilization in the light of his observation that aggression poses civilization's greatest threat – the threat mitigated, however, by people's bonding libidinally as an antidote to the aggression they might otherwise unleash. Civilization, according to the revised definition, is a special process akin to individual development, as Freud maintained before. According to the new view, it unfolds specifically in the service of the life instincts. For it is the life instincts that aim to combine individuals and then families and ever-larger groups into one unity, of humankind. Thus, civilization, threatened by aggression on the one side and perpetuated by Eros on the other, reflects the ongoing struggle between Eros, or life, and death (Freud, 1930, p. 122).[12]

THE ROLE OF GUILT IN THE INHIBITION OF AGGRESSION

Civilization has devised another way of inhibiting aggression, according to Freud. It turns the impulse toward aggression inward, that is transfers it onto the self, whence it manifests as guilt and a corresponding need for punishment – regardless of whether we have actually carried out the impulse. It is the internal constraint on our aggressive impulses that compromises our psychological life, creating the malaise with which Freud perceives humankind to be afflicted.

Development of the capacity for guilt

To feel guilty we need to understand a given act or impulse as bad. Yet we are not born with a sense of good and bad. The external environment initially impresses those values on us; left to our own devices we would distinguish only the agreeable and the painful, as per the pleasure principle.[13] Initially, we understand as bad those acts that might threaten the loss of that love, and we avoid those acts on account of the threat. The individual's mentality at this stage is better described as social anxiety than as a guilty conscience. Thus far, Freud says, the individual's morality extends no further than the fear of punishment and the effort to avoid it; that is the only morality available to children. Not until, as a result of the resolution of the Oedipus complex, we internalize our parents and thereby form a superego, do we attain conscience proper. We reproach ourselves for our intentions, judge our actions before they happen, and punish ourselves accordingly.

[12]   Freud (1930, p. 123) muses briefly on the observation that animals seem not to exhibit the eternal struggle between life and death instincts. They have their pregiven organization and functions and do not strive to break free of their restrictions. They might have struggled earlier and eventually achieved a balance between their instinctual dispositions and environmental influences.

[13]   See the latter part of Chapter 6 here on Freud's paper on Negation (1925a), in which he treats our earliest discriminations along these lines.

Freud finds support for the idea that intentions, and not only acts, can provoke the reproaches of conscience in the observation that fully abstemious people suffer the reproaches. Presumably the temptation – to aggress, for example – increases the more it is held back, and the savagery of the superego increases correspondingly (see Chapters 9 and 10 here).[14]

Therefore, to inhibit, say, an aggressive impulse at the behest of the superego is to provoke one act of aggression while restraining another. We exchange our outward aggressive impulse for an inward-directed one in the form of harsh judgment and punitive battery. Although we may, in doing so, purchase the love of the external authorities, we do so at the price of internal unhappiness.

The severity of the superego revisited

Civilization and its Discontents, then, comes to a focus on the influence on the superego's ferocity of those renounced aggressive impulses that are turned inward. Freud mentioned the possibility of this influence earlier in passing while dwelling on other factors – the perceived severity of the actual parents, the "de-fusion" of the life and death instincts that arises from internalizing the parents (see Chapters 9 and 10 here).[15]

The new emphasis has the advantage, Freud says, that it can account for the unrelenting severity of the superego in some people, which cannot be accounted for by other factors. If the superego's severity only imitated the severity of the parents, for example, then we would expect its severity to remain constant over time, or even

[14]   A similar enhancement of the superego's ferocity exists in the increase in the reproaches of conscience in those of advanced intellectuality, and hence of strong superego development, who experience ill luck. Guilt is the source of the unduly strict commandments of religion. Adherents, by blaming their misfortunes on themselves, avert the need to aggress against God, whose love and favor they fear they might lose. Freud notes the contrast with primitive peoples, who would blame and thrash their fetish, for failing in its duty, rather than punish themselves.

[15]   "De-fusion" refers to the weakening of the hold of the life instincts over the death instinct. When the love object becomes internalized, the life instincts have no opportunity to act at full strength (see Chapter 9).

diminish for lack of fresh input. The same would be true if it reflected the "de-fusion" of instincts arising from the internalization of the parents; that, too, would be a one-time, or one-period, occurrence.

Freud asks us, continuing this line of argument, to assume the renounced instinct on which the superego builds to be an aggressive one; he will justify the assumption shortly. He asks us to assume further that every time people want to lash out at others but refrain from doing so, their superego assails them; they feel guilt or at least some somaticized manifestation of guilt. We would then see that the superego could continue to assail people long after they have internalized their parents and experienced the de-fusion of instincts that results. Indeed, for every aggressive impulse they feel but inhibit, they would experience a fresh assault from the superego. Freud believes, based on the analysis of neurotic patients, who experience especially severe self-reproaches, that something like this occurs. In his later *An Outline of Psychoanalysis* (1940a), he cites circumstantial support for the idea of turning toward the self the aggression people wanted to direct outward. They tear their hair or beat their face with their fist, suggesting, Freud notes, the treatment they wanted to give to someone else (Freud, 1940a, p. 150).

Perhaps, Freud extrapolates further, the superego levels against people the aggression they wanted to unleash against the authorities who thwarted their earliest and hence strongest instincts; they withheld the aggression out of fear of loss of love. Withholding that aggression, the analysis continues, puts children in the "economically difficult" situation of harboring undischarged hostility against those they also love and on whom they depend. The internalization of the parents, which concludes the Oedipal period (see Chapter 9 here), affords one way out of that situation.

As Freud envisions the circumstance, the ego assumes the role of the parents, having incorporated them, and the voice of the superego enters thus: "'If I were the father and you were the child, I should treat you badly'" (Freud, 1930, p. 129). The whole process nets the preservation of harmony with the real parents and the battery of the ego from within, as a consequence of the ego's former, restrained vengefulness.[16]

But Freud thinks the ferocity of the superego exceeds even the level that could be accounted for by either these redirected impulses or the impression of their parents' own severity children may have internalized – and the contribution of the "de-fusion" of instincts that follows upon internalizing a love object (see Chapter 9 here). He perceives an inexplicable ferocity even in babies' and small children's tantrums and other overt behavioral responses to their earliest instinctual frustrations, for instance when they are denied something they want. He tentatively traces the rage of both superego and thwarted child to the phylogenetic model wherein the primal sons resolved their ambivalence toward the father by rising up and killing him (see Chapter 9, Note 7 here).

Primal guilt

A natural progression would have unfolded from there leading to guilt. Although the primal killing would have fulfilled the brothers' aggressive impulses, it would have left no object to satisfy their residual affectionate impulses. Remorse, which requires an actual regrettable deed, arose in its place. That remorse would have produced two outcomes. One is the internalization of the father so as to preserve the relationship with him, as happens at the end of the Oedipal period in all children today and precipitates the formation of the superego. The other is the institution of restraints to prevent repetition of the terrible deed in future generations. But further generations did repeat the deed, or at least aggressed against the father, and, now observed by the superego, those deeds and the impulses behind them provoked the

[16]   From the idea that the superego's ferocity does not follow only the model of the actual parents, Freud derives the generalization that even children raised leniently – spoiled children – may form superegos as strong as those formed by children with strict upbringing. He notes in this connection the suggestion of Franz Alexander (1927) that children with lenient parents may, under the influence of the love they perceive they are receiving, have nowhere to direct their aggression but inward.

sense of guilt. The guilt, in turn, would have intensified with every impulse toward aggressiveness individuals suppressed.

This narrative, however hypothetical, brings out two general and critical features of our moral nature, according to Freud.

One is that love has a role in the creation of conscience. We have a conscience because we internalize, or introject, our lost object. We introject the object because we loved it, and introjection affords a way to preserve it.

The second feature is the inevitability of the sense of guilt, an expression of the conflict born of ambivalence. That conflict arises as soon as humans live together. When the community extends no further than the family, the conflict assumes the form of the Oedipal complex: children want to merge with their parents and also detest them. As soon as the community widens, the conflict continues on a larger scale: aggressive urges follow the combining of humans into ever-larger, closely knit groups. Guilt is brought about by the conflict between those urges and the erotic impulsions built into civilization, itself a by-product of Eros, the impulsion toward unity. The resulting inhibition of aggression will produce a continually increasing sense of guilt that plays out in ever-wider communities and may reach levels the individual can no longer tolerate.

GUILT, INDIVIDUALS, AND CIVILIZATION

Guilt exacts the most problematic toll imposed by civilization, Freud concludes.

Both healthy people and obsessional neurotics experience guilt mostly consciously; individuals with other forms of neurosis may experience guilt unconsciously (see Chapter 6).[17] The pattern may be linked to the circumstance that guilt felt in response to a deed arises consciously, whereas that arising in response to the harboring of an evil impulse may remain unconscious; some neuroses are built on withheld aggressive impulses (see Chapters 1 and 6 here). Ultimately

---

[17]   Guilt may arise unconsciously to some extent in healthy people also. It manifests as an anxiety they experience as a general malaise.

guilt in all of us shades into anxiety, coinciding, when fully developed, with the fear of the superego.

Christianity seems to recognize the play of guilt in daily life in its recognition of sin, on account of which we admit our guilt. It goes further in assuming the possibility of redemption. It envisions redemption to occur through the sacrifice of a single person's life, that person having assumed the guilt common to all. That single life, in turn, may, on the assumption that punishment occurs in kind, represent the murder of another individual, for which we all feel guilty, namely the murder of the primal father (see Freud, 1913b, Chapter IV).

A summary of terms

Freud next undertakes to recapitulate the meaning of the terms that refer to different aspects of this first experience of guilt associated with the killing of the primal father, which, according to him, is the starting point of civilization. The *superego* is an agency he has inferred. It exercises *conscience*, which requires a superego and denotes the watching over and judging of the actions and intentions of the ego. The ego experiences *guilt*, which refers to its perception of a tension between its exertions and the superego's demands. *Remorse* characterizes the ego's reaction when it experiences guilt for an act. It punishes the ego for the act it has committed or expresses a need for punishment.

People can experience guilt and remorse before the formation of conscience and hence of the superego. Prior to the formation of the superego, the two converge, and both refer then to the ego's response to its execution of an act on account of which it feels threatened with the loss of an external authority's love. Guilt, at that stage, assumes the form of fear of that external authority, in other words social anxiety; it reflects the conflict between the impulsion toward satisfying our instincts and the need for the authority's love. After the superego forms, both intended and completed acts can provoke guilt, while only completed acts provoke remorse.

Guilt as a consequence of the inhibition of aggression

Having built the case for the contribution of inhibited aggression to the sense of guilt, Freud explores whether aggression is the only instinctual impulse whose inhibition can form guilt. He, contrary to the thinking of other psychoanalysts of his day that the frustration of any instinctual satisfaction heightens our sense of guilt, surmises the inhibition of only aggression does so. His reasoning is that aggression supplies the very impulsion of which guilt is made, guilt being aggression directed inward.

Frustrated erotic demands, by contrast, would fail to supply that impulsion. Such demands, like unrequited lust for the mother or sexual needs left unfulfilled by the impotence of a spouse, would produce only unspent libido – sexual energy with nowhere to go. They would not produce a current of aggression that could then turn back on the self. The frustrated erotic urges could provoke – as opposed to automatically yield – aggression, which, if withheld, could in turn materialize into guilt.

Unfulfilled erotic demands do, however, follow a further trajectory and may appear as neurotic symptoms. Freud has long observed neurotic symptoms to express unfulfilled erotic wishes. In his *Introductory Lectures on Psychoanalysis* (1917a, Lecture 17, pp. 261–263), for example, he describes an obsessive patient who followed the ritual each morning of dashing from her room to an adjoining one, where she stood by a table and summoned her maid; she then either dispatched the maid on a minor errand or dismissed her, while she returned to her room.

Analysis revealed she was re-enacting the scene of her wedding night, on which her husband, after running several times to her room, had proved impotent. The couple separated subsequently and now, ten years later, was contemplating a divorce. The patient, when she ran to the table in the adjoining room during her ritual, always stood next to a large stain on the tablecloth, which her maid would have had to see when she answered her mistress' call. By means of this behavior, her symptom, she corrected the scene of her wedding night, providing her husband's virility and allowing the maid to see its results.

Civilization and the struggle between the life and death instincts for supremacy

Freud, in closing, takes up the analogy between individual development and that of civilization that has threaded through *Civilization and its Discontents*. Both the process of civilization and individual development represent the modification of organic life, instigated by the exigencies of reality, or necessity, under the influence of the life instincts. Necessity forces us, in both, to make accommodations so as to assure our individual and species survival: we learn to delay gratification and take account of our surroundings in the case of individual development[18] and develop tool use and collaborative work in the case of cultural development.[19] The life instincts guide these efforts in pressing us toward unification into a community bound by libidinal ties.

Both individual and cultural development, consistent with the analogy between them, include a striving toward individual happiness governed by the pleasure principle and aimed toward union with the community. However, individual development gives individual happiness priority and realizes the urge toward community mainly in the form of restrictions on the individual; civilization, in contrast, necessarily relegates individual happiness to the background and drives principally toward creating and sustaining community.

Freud, extending the analogy further, wonders whether communities, like individuals, might not develop a superego. The communal superego would derive not from a literal father, but from the impressions left by a succession of prominent leaders. The leaders would include individuals with great presence of mind and strong and defined impulses. Like the putative primal father, they might have met disparagement and maltreatment, including murder, during their

---

[18]   This dynamic is captured by Freud's account of the emergence of the reality principle (see Chapter 2 here).

[19]   See earlier this chapter for the account of cultural development.

lifetime and became venerated afterward. The cultural superego also, like the individual superego, establishes strict ethical demands, in consequence of which the community suffers the drubbing of conscience.

In civilization, as in individual neurosis, the superego makes overly strict demands on the ego, Freud believes, not least because it takes too little account of the individual's happiness. The cultural superego disregards the natural mental constitution of humans and assumes that constitution can carry out any task required of it. However, the overly strong demands will only produce a revolt or neurosis. Freud wonders whether in time whole cultures will become neurotic, as individuals have done. Granted, we would find it difficult to discern such a progression, because no healthy model would exist to compare it to.[20]

Freud remarks the ubiquity of the formula that pits the life and death instincts against each other in both the process of civilization and individual development, as well as in organic life in general. He declines to pass judgment on the value of civilization. He wants to impart only that it is not unqualifiedly good and precious. The question remains open of whether cultural development will prove able to master the disturbance caused by inward and outward aggression. At the time Freud wrote, near the outbreak of World War II, the human race had developed the capacity to destroy itself. The circumstance may have contributed to the broad unrest, unhappiness, and anxiety he observed. He wonders whether the life instincts would be able to reassert themselves and tip the balance back the other way.

---

[20]   Freud suspects a change in the relation of humans to private property would do more to counteract aggression than can any ethical demand (1930, p. 143). As he cautioned earlier (see Note 9, this chapter), however, the maneuver will work only if we remain realistic about human nature. Aggression will need to find an outlet, somewhere.

Epilogue: What Freud really meant

Erik Erikson, the esteemed cultural psychologist and psychoanalyst, once bristled at what he called Freud's "originology" (1958, p. 18). He was referring to a way of thought that attempts to understand every human condition by tracing it to an earlier and simpler state, ultimately the earliest and simplest state, to which the condition might relate. Erikson himself believed, to the contrary, that later-emerging forms of experience add something new to existing structure, and that the two interact dialectically. For him, present and past, like culture and the individual or the social and biological, create one another; for example, through subtle variations in child-rearing, cultures help to shape the kinds of individuals who can function effectively within them, as he famously documented in his *Childhood and Society* (1950).

Erikson is one among many psychoanalytic theorists after Freud who have understood him to have reduced mental life in this way to one or another of its elements. They insist, for example, humans are not the mere hedonists they understand Freud's pleasure principle to imply they are (e.g., Fairbairn, 1994, Vol. 1, p. 131). Or they say the full panoply of adult passions and pursuits cannot be reduced to sexual or aggressive drives or to the conflicts they precipitate (e.g., Hartmann, 1939; Kohut, 1977). Some maintain that Freud's compartmentalization of the way the mind operates engenders loss of agency, when we need desperately to reverse such loss should we fall ill (e.g., Schafer, 1976). Others fault Freud for underestimating the positive potential inherent in the early mental stages he emphasizes, like narcissism (e.g., Kohut, 1977).

Freud does seek to trace human mental life to its primordial constituents. He indeed declares the avoidance of pain and cultivation of pleasure – the pleasure principle – to be the initial and most fundamental rule of our mental life (Freud, 1911; Chapter 2 here). He traces the principle to the most primitive possible behavior, the reflex; he traces the reflex, in turn, to the original function of the nervous system, which is to discharge the excitation that reaches it (Freud, 1900; Chapter 2 here). He identifies sex and, as of his earlier writings, survival, as the most basic instincts from which all impulses derive (1915a; Chapter 5 here). He subsequently (1920; Chapter 8 here) adds the death instinct to the group: "Death," he says, quoting Schopenhauer, is the "true result and to that extent the purpose of life."[1] Ten years later, in *Civilization and its Discontents* (1930; Chapter 11 here), he segues from the death instinct to aggression, yet another pivot around which the mind, and civilization, turn.

But these kernels of Freud's theory hold a place opposite to the position often ascribed to them. He uses them not to reduce our mental life to its points of origin or root impulses, but to build a theory of the human mind from first principles.

Distortion of Freud's theory begins with his psychoanalytic successors, whose misreadings have colored both the popular and scholarly representation of it. In response to their experience treating ever-widening patient-populations, those practitioners introduced refinements of the theory at the expense of a distortion of its original tenets. The discussion that follows does not address their valuable clinical contributions. Rather, it juxtaposes their broadly adopted assertions about Freud's theory with what he actually meant in order to set into relief the pillars of the theory as it stood at the end of his life.

The field of psychoanalysis continued to grow after Freud, principally in two directions. One, exemplified by the Ego Psychology movement, turned from what practitioners perceived as Freud's emphasis on uncovering primal urges – the id – toward what he distinguished as ego, the arbiter between our inner life and the external world. The other direction, exemplified by the Object Relations

---

[1] On p. 50; p. 236 in A. Schopenhauer, 1851, *Sämtliche Werke*, 5, ed. Hübscher, Leipzig, 1938. See Chapter 8 here.

school, to which the emphasis on ego function naturally segued, focused specifically on the ego's relation to others as against Freud's perceived emphasis on its intrapsychic, not other-directed, dynamics. Both approaches have grown more elaborate and more nuanced over time, with the two intertwining more often than not, each rejecting elements of Freud's thought it has misinterpreted.

ON THE PRIORITY OF THE PLEASURE PRINCIPLE

With respect to Freud's claim of the existence of a universal pleasure principle, subsequent psychoanalytic theorists have argued we arrive in the world wired for purposes other than the satisfaction of simple pleasures. Central among those purposes, according to them, is social interaction.

René Spitz (1965), for example, maintained that babies, aside from any pleasure-seeking impulse they may have, naturally incline toward establishing a connection with others. The position is echoed by later Attachment theorists beginning with John Bowlby (1969) and continuing with modern investigators of the mother–infant relationship, e.g., Daniel Stern (1985).

W.R.D. Fairbairn (1994, p. 131ff), of the British Object Relations school, rejected what he viewed as Freud's "hedonic" premise on a similar basis. We do not seek first and foremost to gratify our urges, using others as a means for the purpose, Fairbairn said; we seek connection with them as an end in itself. Pleasure might be one form, perhaps the most desired form, of connecting with others. However, he contends, we will retain connections by other means if we must. Thus, for instance, abused children willingly repeat painful experiences if doing so will preserve the bond with their significant others, instead of seeking an alternative object who might supply pleasure rather than pain.

Fairbairn's observations retain importance especially to therapy, which, he recognized, needs to go beyond facilitating insight into the addictiveness of abusive relationships to demonstrating the feasibility of an alternative. But those who see either these observations or their therapeutic implications as undercutting the primacy of the pleasure principle err in two significant ways.

First, even within the compass of the pleasure principle, Freud was no stranger to the idea that people might actively seek experiences that would seem to others to bring only pain. He addresses the point directly in his paper on masochism (1924; Chapter 10 here), as well as in earlier discussions of the pleasure principle (e.g., 1900, 1909a, 1917a; Chapter 2 here). The latter include his writings on dreams and neuroses, in which he insists that even the most horrific nightmares and the most debilitating symptoms have a payoff.

The very notion that symptoms have a sense, a theme of Freud's *Five Lectures* (Chapter 1 here), flows directly from the stipulation of the pleasure principle. A compulsive hand-washer, for example, on Freud's analysis, might turn out to be "washing" something other than literal dirt from his hands, perhaps guilt for an early imagined transgression he cannot acknowledge. Insofar as a symptom addresses some purpose, it settles a need; in settling a need, it relieves the need, and to relieve a need is to produce pleasure. This framework easily accommodates Fairbairn's observation that children may cling to caregivers who abuse them and repeat the pattern later on.

The preceding challenges err in a second way in their assumption that Freud, in recognizing the priority we grant the avoidance of pain and cultivation of pleasure, meant we live only for our pleasures. As he makes clear in *Two Principles in Mental Functioning* (1911; Chapter 2 here), the pleasure principle is the first of *two* building blocks of a human mind. Were we governed by the pleasure principle exclusively we would quickly die. To run into the middle of the street because it's more fun than waiting for the light might result in our being hit by a truck; to hallucinate satiety because of its immediate comfort would leave us to starve. But our minds are also constructed to search, register, experiment with, and store information from the external world, and as such to function according to a *reality*, as well as a *pleasure*, principle.

However, even if the striving for pleasure is universal, the early ego psychologist Heinz Hartmann (1939) rejected, as have many other commentators, that striving – essentially the discharge of our needs – as a developmental starting point. Hartmann holds instead that we are born with latent perception, language, thinking, and other ego functions that facilitate the mind's engagement with the outside world. Should the environment in which we find ourselves prove hospitable, these pregiven adaptive capabilities then unfold as a matter of course – not as part of a circuitous route to the satisfaction of frustrated needs.

No one, including Freud, would take issue with the idea that our cognitive capabilities may by this point in our evolution be to some degree built in and that they likely flower in a nurturing surround (e.g., Freud, 1940a, p. 185). It is important to understand why he grants developmental priority nonetheless, not to the unfolding of those capabilities, but to the dictates of the pleasure principle.

Were it not for the "decision"[2] (Freud, 1911, p. 219), as Freud puts it, to form a conception of the real, we might never have developed perception, memory, the senses, and action – the bulwarks of our cognitive system. And, were it not for the need to restrain motor discharge so as to convert it into effective action, we would not have formed thought. This vision is the opposite of the conventional wisdom and tacitly Hartmann's. Those viewpoints interpret these capabilities as having come about as a result of the evolutionary pressure to detect and avoid danger and to discern and pursue advantages to our survival.[3]

Freud would not dispute the conventional wisdom that sees us as retaining behaviors that favor survival. But his vision breaks that scenario down in an enlightening, and ultimately coherent, way.

Pleasure and pain, Freud says, are more primordial psychologically than are specific sensory qualities. Their primacy is reflected in

---

[2]   *entschliessen*

[3]   Freud's assertion here of the primacy of the pleasure principle via a vision in which we at some point "decide" to distinguish and abide by actual, rather than fantasied, reality dovetails enlighteningly with the observation of neurosis from which he launches paper on the two principles (see Chapter 2 here). Neurosis, he says, has the result, and therefore presumably the aim, of withdrawing the sufferer from reality. The afflicted must, if they are to recover, *decide* to evaluate whether, for example, the threat of germs that is about to motivate yet another cycle of handwashing is real and to take appropriate action if it is not real.

the original purpose of the nervous system to discharge stimuli, that purpose associated with relief, or pleasure.

The simplest conceivable psychological organization would have only that function, to discharge the stimuli that impinge on it. For an organism to carry out the discharge it would not need to know the source of, or anything else about, the stimuli; it would just discharge what disturbed it. That organism would not last, because in being unable to distinguish between helpful and harmful stimuli, it would not be able to prevent itself from destruction. Therefore, the only organisms that exist are those with some "reality" function and the equipment for carrying it out.

The reverse scenario, in which an organism had sensory or action capabilities independent of the urge toward discharge – i.e., observed no pleasure principle – has no coherence. That is because, in the absence of something like an urge toward discharge, it would have no incentive to detect anything or to act. Freud's pleasure principle provides the incentive, and he reasonably conceives it as the more basic psychical function.[4]

ON INSTINCTS AS THE MOTIVATIONAL BASIS
OF MENTAL LIFE

Freud introduces the idea of instinct to characterize the impetus that presses the pleasure principle – the striving toward stimulus reduction[5] – into action. Commentators on Freud have disparaged his apparent depiction of humans as bundles of bestial impulses – "drives" – gradually harnessed at the behest of outside forces.[6] They

[4] Melanie Klein (e.g., 1957), in her vision of babies' initial universe – the "good breast" vs. the "bad breast," or simply the good vs. the bad – evokes the pleasure principle. Her vision aligns with the idea that initially we want to "eat it" or "spit it out" (Freud, 1925a, p. 237; Chapter 6 here): we like it, or we dislike it, and if we dislike it, we want to be rid of it. That determination takes priority, for both Klein and Freud, over ego functions like the recognition of "objects" Hartmann wants to endow us with.

[5] Freud (e.g., 1924, 1930; Chapters 10 and 11 here) eventually adds the possibility of our gaining pleasure from an increase in stimulus. Although he accordingly modifies his definition of pleasure, the drive toward stimulus reduction remains paramount.

[6] I follow the relevant authors' usage in citing "drives" here, rather than "instincts," for Freud's *Triebe*. I otherwise use "instincts," following the English translation in the

see drives instead as derivative of or reactive to experience (e.g., Hartmann, 1939; Jacobson, 1964; Kernberg, 1976) or contend that object relations, not drives, fill the core of our emotional life (see Mahler, 1968; Klein, 1957; Bion, 1962; Kohut, 1984; Erikson, 1950). Along similar lines, some commentators protest what they see as Freud's reduction of the 'higher and finer' in mental life to those drives (e.g., Hartmann, 1939; Loewald, 1988). Others object to the evident denigration of the social other to the mere instrument of them (e.g., Spitz, 1965; Fairbairn, 1952; Bion, 1962).

Hartmann (1939), in conceiving development as the progressive unfolding of endowed adaptive capabilities of the ego – including, as just noted, perception, language, thinking, and the concept of objects – observed that those capabilities do not inherently embody Freud's drives, sex and aggression.[7] They must therefore, Hartmann reasoned, become attached to drives contingently; speech, for example, could become compromised by instinctual conflict and give way to stuttering.

Edith Jacobson (1964), similarly, conceived Freud's drives as only potential at birth, ready to be triggered into existence by experience, which determines the form they take once they emerge. Colored by good or bad experience, they turn more toward love and positive motivation or more toward aggression and destruction. Otto Kernberg (1976) also conceives the drives as potential and reactive, contingent on our capacity to experience good and bad states. When babies have pleasurable and gratifying experiences they want to recreate them, and when they experience pain and frustration they want to do away with their source. The former experiences propagate libidinal, or sexual, interests, and the latter, aggressive ones.

> *Standard Edition of the Complete Psychological Works of Sigmund Freud* (J. Strachey, Ed. and Trans.). "Instinct" picks up the sense of a boundary concept between psychology and biology intended by Freud. "Drive," according to some of the authors who use it, conveys the unmediated quality of impulse that Freud also intends, without the suggestion of the narrow connotation of fixed action pattern in animals common in contemporary biological usages (e.g., Lear, 2000; Mitchell & Black, 1995).
>
> [7]   Although Freud equivocates about the primacy of aggression as a basal instinct (see the next section of this chapter), the misrepresentation of his categorization does not affect the argument that follows in this section.

Self Psychologist Heinz Kohut contended people have a primary urge toward growth, sex and aggression arising only as byproducts of disintegration of the self. Thus, for example, masturbation among sufferers of such disintegration might represent not the vigorous pursuit of unobstructed sexuality, but a joyless effort merely to feel alive (1979, p. 425). Likewise, aggression in those individuals might connote not the release of an innate urge to destroy, but a post-traumatic protective measure undertaken to hold further trauma at bay.

Margaret Mahler (1968), among the first of many to replace "drives" with object relations as our emotional center, saw, instead of drives gradually shaped by experience, a being growing in complexity and independence. Her signature work on infants' patterns of separation and individuation confirmed her view that symbiosis with the mother confers on developing individuals the capacity for ever greater differentiation from her. Melanie Klein (1957), the later Kleinian analyst Wilfred Bion (1962), and the British Object Relations school that grew from Klein's work (e.g., Fairbairn, 1952) developed in different ways the idea that we are born with an impetus toward relationship independent of any intrinsic drives in the Freudian sense.

John Bowlby (1969), extending this last tradition to theory and research outside psychoanalysis, believed we arrive with our instincts preadapted to a distinctly human environment and honed to that end over millions of years by natural selection. We are born with a disposition to attach – an instinctual tendency to form and retain a deep bond with the mother – which transcends the gratification of our physical needs. A line of evidence supporting that primacy, to which Bowlby alludes, is the finding that babies will form attachments to the mother even when she is not the person meeting their basic needs – for example when a wet nurse assumes that responsibility (e.g., Schaeffer and Emerson, 1964). It is this evolution, not the bestial impulses in the raw Freud was misinterpreted to have imagined, that represents our connection to the animal world.

Commentary on Freud's apparent reduction of the so-called higher and finer to basal drives, and of the love object to but fodder for the drives, flows from the foregoing ideas about his general discussion of drives (instincts).

With respect to the former, Hartmann (1939), believing our higher ego functions show no inherent sign of Freud's primordial drives, maintained our intellectual and cultural achievements could not have arisen by sublimation of those drives. Later interests such as photography or scientific research, or the striving toward mastery in one's field, might, he thought, represent denuded and thoroughly transformed voyeurism or aggression, respectively. But any continuity they expressed had to involve more than a redirection, i.e., sublimation, of those sources. Hans Loewald (1988), echoing Hartmann, believed such later interests exhibited features so novel they could not be traced to infantile sexuality or aggression even if those drives were stripped of their intensity and rechanneled in a socially acceptable way.

With respect to the conception of the love object, Freud's characterization, originally in "Instincts and their vicissitudes" (1915a; Chapter 5 here), of babies' love objects as constituents of their instincts has drawn rebukes especially from commentators in the Object Relations tradition. That characterization has led many to understand him to have said others serve only as a means to gratify babies' urges. They believe, on the contrary, as we have seen, babies instead seek a connection with others for its own sake (e.g., Bion, 1984; Bowlby, 1969; Fairbairn, 1952; Spitz, 1965).

All of these reservations concerning Freud's ideas about instincts on the part of Freud's successors draw upon a misreading of Freud's theory of instincts. Freud did not intend his delineation of basic instincts to reduce humans to beasts or to depict their life trajectory as the struggle to rein in bestial urges. He did not reduce humans' higher and finer achievements to sexual instinct in tracing their origin there. And he did not claim babies' primary others serve only as the vehicle through which instinctual satisfaction arises. Lastly, for all the concern with Freud's apparent reduction of mental life to primary instincts, the foregoing reservations somewhat misrepresent what Freud understood those instincts to be.

"Bestial" urges

Far from reducing humans to beasts, Freud was attempting to identify building blocks of the mind so basic they trace all the way back to our animal ancestors. He stipulated that the nervous system seeks first and foremost to discharge the tensions that arise within it (see Chapter 2 here). If that imperative precipitates our most rudimentary impulsions, then the question follows of what produces an impelling tension. Freud answers, "instinct," or stimuli generated organically from within. Those stimuli, by contrast with external stimuli, do not easily find discharge and therefore make a high demand upon the mind: whereas we can in a single act withdraw from the pain of a cold external surface, we cannot with direct action eliminate an internal stimulus like hunger or the longing for a beloved other.

He then wants to know which kinds of instincts exist that reduce to no simpler constituents. In "Instincts and their vicissitudes" (1915a; Chapter 5 here) he makes a strong case for the primacy and irreducibility of "sexual" and "self-preservative" instincts. He cites their dedication, respectively, to preservation of the species and preservation of the individual and their capacity for conflict. Regarding their capacity for conflict, if the two different classes of urges can conflict with one another, then they must be separate.

Those who disparage Freud's emphasis on instincts over adaptive capabilities like babies' cognitive apparatus or their connection with objects set up false dichotomies. In emphasizing instincts, Freud is attempting to specify the architecture of the system. He is not saying what is important in life. Instincts and all they become make the system go.

When commentators characterize Freud's view of human endeavor as a struggle to contain drives, as opposed to as a reduction to them, they overlook an important element of the containment we perform. The cardinal way in which we contain our drives – to the extent we contain them – namely by repression, vastly exceeds what a beast does when it grapples with its confinement. To come to the fears – of abandonment, of a loss of self-regard – that drive repression is a decidedly human process.

But containing our drives is not our dominant program, according to Freud. The object of the individual life is to *satisfy* its instinctual demands, not to deny them (Freud, 1909a, pp. 54–55;1940a, p. 148). Our individual psychology is built around that calling. As a clinician Freud dedicated himself to helping patients uncover impulses they had desperately controlled and cut off – repressed – and the cost of having done so. He left patients with three options, only one of which was to repudiate – consciously – the now-exposed impulse. The other two were, respectively, to redirect the impulse or to embrace it.

The possibility of the "higher and finer"

Freud, in ascribing our intellectual and cultural achievements to the sublimation of our root instincts, was not reducing those achievements to the instincts. In postulating the continuities he did, he pointed out the very richness others would deny his account. His argument is that if all our strivings ultimately derive from, let us say, sexual or ego (self-preservative) instincts, then we ought to be able to identify traces of either or both impulsions in all human endeavor.

The particular connections Freud draws between earlier impulses and later attainments are persuasive, not least because they make sense. For example, under his ascription of our impulses to the sexual or ego instincts, curiosity and theatrical display would seem to affiliate more naturally with the so-called sexual pole of the dichotomy than with the survival pole: we do not need curiosity to survive.[8] Within that

---

8   In a late letter to Marie Bonaparte (Jones, 1957, vol. 3, pp. 464–465, Letter #33, May 27, 1937), Freud suggests a derivation of scientific curiosity, as manifested in the disposition to research, from sublimated aggressive instinct, which had not entered his theory when he wrote earlier, in 1909a, of a connection between curiosity and libido. To investigate, he later writes, is to analyze, or to take apart, and aggression embodies the undoing of things. Freud does not reconcile the two accounts; we may note they are not incompatible.

frame, furthermore, scopophilia and exhibitionism, as sexual instincts specifically of childhood, do not contribute to the sexual act or any other external function; like the rest of infantile sexuality, they are purely for enjoyment in and of themselves. The same is true of curiosity and also of our impetus to display something of ourselves, theatrically or artistically, to others. It is not a stretch to see the potential for adult curiosity and wonderment in a child's propensity to look at another's naked body and become fascinated by it.

The power of Freud's analysis is perhaps even better reflected in his passing commentary on beauty in *Civilization and its Discontents* (1930; see Chapter 11, Note 1 here). Beauty, he says, has a mildly intoxicating quality whose origin is elusive. He wonders whether our capacity to be moved by it – whether the stirrings we feel – might not trace ultimately to the field of sexual feeling. Historically, he suggests, beauty might have evolved as a property attaching to secondary sexual characteristics, such as the face or the figure, those designed to attract, as opposed to those evolved to serve the sexual act in itself. Freud, although easily misread – again reductively – to have claimed there is something sexual about what we find beautiful (e.g., Beigel, 1953), is among the few who have raised, let alone grappled with, the question of where the sensibility might have come from.

In other instances in which Freud anchors prizes of our civilized state in root impulses like sexuality, his argument is anything but reductive in its recognition of the complexity of those acquisitions. Other investigators commonly do not acknowledge the depth and texture of marks of civilized life such as shame, disgust, and morality. Freud, however, envisioned a path leading from coprophilia through the repression of anal sexuality in the case of shame and disgust, and from the Oedipal complex through its repression in the case of morality (see Chapters 1 and 9 here). Freud's account of the depth and texture, regardless of one's view of its substance, makes clear that these characteristics are not simple, spontaneous, or taught.

Finally, sublimation itself is, in Freud's conception, an impelling force toward development, not the conservative or regressive one implied by criticisms of it as reductive. We sublimate an impulse when the prospect of its realization alarms us, despite our simultaneously existing desire to realize it. In sublimating it, we change its form. Indeed sublimation succeeds best when it finds a pathway not yet taken, so the impulse it is shielding can continue to escape notice. Much of the ongoing proliferation of our intellectual, aesthetic, and cultural activity confers no practical advantage or inherent pleasure over what came before. It therefore could not be fully explained by the operation of "external disturbing and diverting influences" (Freud, 1920, p. 38), one of the few remaining motors of development Freud's later theory allows. Sublimation, driven from within, can fill the breach, thus providing an impelling force for developments we would be hard pressed to account for in other ways.

The social other as object of instinct

Freud's specification that instincts depend on objects to achieve their aim forms part of his definition of "instinct." It does not equate to the declaration that others do no more than afford a means to gratify babies' urges. Freud was mapping out the requisites of an instinct; among others, it must have an object. He was not answering the question, "On what does babies' successful development depend?" His main theoretical interest lay in the details of the interior processes by which the mind negotiates its circumstances once the factors that bring them about are in play.[9]

Whereas Freud's successors appear to have devoted themselves to the extraction of causes of illness, Freud pursued the internal dynamic that allows the causes to have the effect they do. If a person

---

[9] Freud (1940a, p. 185) did address the determinants of successful development in a general way, by pointing to the delicate interplay of constitution, experience, environment, and the generic pressures of living in human society in determining a person's mental health. He (1910) noted in that connection the impact of Leonardo's early abandonment by his father on Leonardo's later trajectory, allowing that damage to the ego could precipitate a neurosis or at least upset healthy psychological functioning. Through numerous interstitial steps he infers that Leonardo's father's early neglect later emerged in Leonardo's abandonment of individual artistic works and eventually his art altogether.

falls ill of forces obstructing the person's ego development, as per the account of later writers, the illness contains some dynamic that keeps it going. That dynamic may entail the interplay of forces Freud depicts: unrequited longing, undischarged aggression, or jealousy – and the intense fear of loss of the loved other should any of those impulses find expression; to those forces we may add their sequelae in processes like repression and formations like the superego.

Freud's root instincts and the place of aggression in them

Scholarly and popular conceptions alike of Freud's theory have misconstrued not only the place in the theory, but also the identity, of the instincts Freud took to be basic. Those instincts are pervasively misunderstood to be sex and aggression (see Mitchell and Black, 1995, p. xvii). Freud initially designated the sexual and ego, or self-preservative, instincts as primary and later subsumed both under the broader heading of the *Eros* or life instincts, which he held act in opposition to the death instinct, or *Thanatos*.

Designating sex and aggression as the two root categories of instinct misses half the compass of Freud's own terms, life and death. The life instincts subsume the individual thrust toward living as well as the creation of life via sex and the creation of other unities of individuals, like communities and civilization. The death instinct incorporates any coming apart, that by disintegration, as well as by force; consistent with the process of disintegration the death instinct also subsumes any drift toward quietude or inertness, whether or not the drift is headed toward death.

Aggression, specifically, although increasingly prominent in Freud's theorizing and acknowledged as "original" and "self-subsisting" by the time he writes *Civilization and its Discontents* (1930, p.122), appears throughout his writings as derivative of other instincts. Its derivative status receives clear expression as late as his final summary of his theory, *An Outline of Psychoanalysis* (1940a, pp. 149–150).

In his earlier works, when he recognizes only the sexual and ego instincts, he classes aggression with the sexual instincts on account of its nearness to sadism (Freud, 1915a; Chapter 5 here). Later he rejects that coupling, unable to envision how the impulse to destroy the love object could come from the libido (Freud, 1920, 1923, 1930; Chapters 8, 9, and 11 here).

The death instinct, by now articulated, provides a more natural foundation. In that conception, aggression represents the expulsion outward, under the influence of the life instincts, of destructive tendencies housed in the initially undifferentiated ego–id. Subsequent writers almost universally overlook these relationships, positing aggression, and not the death instinct, as primary, in Freud's name or otherwise (e.g., Hartmann, 1939; Jacobson, 1964; Kohut, 1977).

Freud, in deriving aggression from the death instinct, does face the substantial task of explaining how the death instinct, which denotes the passive drift toward expiration, could give rise to aggression, which embodies activity. He offers that the life instincts, themselves quintessentially active, attach to the death instinct and deflect it outward;[10] in that process of deflection, Freud says, it engages the musculature (Freud, 1923, p 41; Chapter 9 here). Either circumstance – the involvement of the life instincts or the engagement of the musculature – might supply the energic base of aggression.[11]

---

[10]   Some findings in modern biology document a threat of disintegration at the start of new life that must be counteracted by an opposing force for the organism to survive (McIsaac, Huang, Sengupta, & Wingreen, 2011).

[11]   Jonathan Lear (2000), who appreciates Freud's intent, decries what he sees as a portrayal of aggression as a mere defense against the self-destruction that would otherwise arise from the death instinct. Aggression, too ubiquitous to serve in so secondary a role, Lear thinks, might instead arise from a separate source. That source, he suggests, borrowing from Klein (1957/1975), might be a more active, primitive self-destructive trend that could contain the potential for aggression against others (Lear, 2005, p. 162 and Note 27, pp. 242–243).

Freud, in what might seem a related conception, mentions parenthetically in his late An Outline of Psychoanalysis (1940a) that he has no term comparable to libido to denote the "energy" of the destructive instinct (p. 150). In referring to "energy," he seems to imply a process with just such a force to it, as opposed to the passive depletion or decomposition introduced in Beyond the Pleasure Principle (1920). However, it is the passive conception, of a trend toward decomposition and decay, Freud imputes as primary in the works in which he builds his notion of a death instinct and derives aggression from it. That derivation does not, as we have seen, prevent him from allowing that aggression may be inborn by now.

Whether or not this speculative sketch could ground a thorough-going theory of aggression, aggression is not one of the basal tendencies of mental life according to Freud. Those are, again, the drift toward quiescence, ultimately death, and a clamoring for life. Although dying is not an aim in the sense in which living is – it is rather the end toward which all life inexorably moves – we live to live, as well as to die. Aggression, interestingly, even when directed toward utter destruction, is, to Freud, an amalgam of the trends toward living and dying, however much it may be dominated by one of them and regardless of its present self-subsisting status.

ON ORIGINS AND DEVELOPMENT

The charge of originology – the claim that Freud's extrapolation to the origin of our traits reduces us to those origins – misconstrues his intent. Freud anchors all later states and behaviors in their point of origin to show how they are possible. In accord with that program he demonstrates how simple operating principles, such as to repeat what works and avoid what does not, propel us toward the consummate attainments that define us today. In diametric opposition to the idea that we reduce to our origins, Freud's entire theory is about how we move beyond minimal beginnings toward those attainments. Its root idiom is development.

All the criticisms of Freud's theory that see in it a construal of human mentality as little more than its basal impulses converge on the idea that Freud, in searching for our origins, saw little else. Instead Freud is saying that where something comes from is part of what it is. Knowledge of that origin demystifies the later attainment. Thus, for example, at Freud's hands, the peculiar quality of moral impulsion and moral feeling have a base – in the mix of love, hostility, and compulsion produced by the resolution of the Oedipal conflict into the super-ego. On account of that construal we may appreciate a dimension of morality unaddressed by standard approaches.

Development is built into the theory even where Freud might seem to deny its priority, as he might appear to do when he posits in

Beyond the Pleasure Principle that no instinct exists toward development. He says there is only an urge inherent in organic life to repeat
previous states since abandoned (1920, p. 36; Chapter 8 here). He
assumes, recognizing his position as extreme, it is only by dint of the
press of external disturbing forces that change occurs at all. In the
absence of such external forces, he suggests, we would continue to
repeat previous behaviors – gaze voyeuristically, aggress, dominate
and possess, or carry out any other instinctual or acquired behavior.[12]

But, as we have seen Freud also argue (e.g., 1911), life can evolve
significantly as a result of its encounters with those external forces
(see earlier this chapter and also Chapter 2). Our experience of the
nonsatisfaction of our earliest needs prompts the development of the
means necessary to meet them, including the discernment of the real
as opposed to the not-real and the external as opposed to the internal.
These are functions of the ego (Freud, 1911, 1915a, 1923; Chapters 2, 5,
and 9 here), which, together with later experience, bring about the
capacity for repression and sublimation; repression in its turn occasions, among other consequences, a sharp separation of conscious and
unconscious mentation. With repression in place, when our lusts and
longings encounter either external obstruction or internal defense in
the form of the Oedipal crisis, we internalize the parents and form a
superego and its sequelae, like morality. Some interests and impulses
may regroup via sublimation into something different. That line of
development may continue indefinitely, accounting ultimately for
the ever more intricate and nuanced intellectual, aesthetic, and cultural forms we see today.

Mental "compartmentalization" and agency

Freud's tripartite division of mental processes into id, ego, and superego, which superseded his earlier, simpler delineation of conscious

---

[12]   The gazing and aggressing represent the "instincts" of scopophilia and sadism, respectively, Freud describes in "Instincts and their vicissitudes" (1915a; Chapter 5 here);
dominating and possessing refer to Oedipal lust described in *The Ego and the Id* (1923;
Chapter 9 here) and elsewhere.

and unconscious operation, attests to the embeddedness of development in his theory. The three interests emerge sequentially, based on our experience, the latter two adding dimensions to what we see, feel, and do in the world that far exceed our alleged instinctual origins.

Critics have objected that Freud's division of the mind into different forces – id, ego, and superego – dehumanizes the subject. The result, among others, is the disempowerment of the person as agent of his or her experience. Roy Schafer (1976), for example, says the loss of agency communicated by Freud's schema is the very problem from which patients under analysis suffer. They have been disappointed, crushed, and manipulated by forces they have no hope of commanding. They need to learn they *can* control what happens to them and how they experience it.

The intent of Freud's schema is the opposite of that scenario. It is to reflect nuances within an agency he strives to have patients reclaim. The criticism misreads his labeling of id, ego, and superego as objectifying our selves and eviscerating our independent personae, rather than as a schematic identification of the different interests that vie for expression in our minds. It is that schematic convenience that allows Freud to explain how our behavior beyond our early years arises and assumes its distinguishing individual color.

Schafer's view reifies the very construct Freud used to depict us as whole human beings, who, however, are only variably able to move with a unified will. Freud would not be the first to have observed that variability, as centuries of western philosophy attest. He attempted to pinpoint the locus of our internal schisms and used the schematic of id, ego, and superego to do so. From there he aimed, in designing the therapy he did, to give us command over the different forces in our mind and the world around us. He wanted patients to find their way to impulses and impressions they had denied and identify the forces that had brought about the denial – so they could choose among different pathways to healing.

Development and neurosis as based in conflict

Successors to Freud have been unsettled by the primacy he attributes to conflict in our mental life – that primacy flowing from his conception that different interests indeed vie within us. According to many who followed him, Freud saw conflict everywhere, as the motor of normal mental development (e.g., Hartmann, 1939, p. 24) and in the formation of pathology (e.g., Winnicott, 1965). Hartmann (1939), for one, believed a view more consonant with clinical experience would ascribe normal development not to the consequences of conflict but, as he did, to the gradual unfolding of innate adaptations to the parental environment; he contended those adaptations become activated when the parental environment is adequately nurturing. Pathology, according to that view, would arise from the arresting of development brought about by insufficient parenting: when parents fail to meet children's ego needs, the ego fails to grow (e.g., Winnicott, 1965).

Although inadequate parenting may dispose its victims to arrested development, the correlation does not in itself explain how such circumstances translate into disorder. Freud's dissection of internal conflict does do so, however. Let us suppose with Freud and many since that children in inadequately nurturing environments might evolve strategies for surviving in that environment, repeating whatever behavior appeared to assure the continued love of their caregiver. Strategies such as answering to a needy parent's whims can breed conflict within children, who might become torn between their striving to fulfill their own desires and a competing fear of the consequence of refusing the parent. That conflict, Freud concluded based on close analysis of patients' symptoms, may be what ultimately maneuvers pathological formations into place (see Chapter 1 here).

Narcissism and development

Commentators have disparaged Freud not only for his perceived reduction of our higher mental accoutrements to their origins but also, paradoxically, for his apparent disdain for the origins. Here again they misconstrue his intent. His treatment of narcissism is a case in point.

Early narcissism as a positive force in mental life

Some have questioned what they see as Freud's construal of narcissism as an infantile stage we must relinquish (Kohut, 1977). They regard the stage instead as a period of potential meaning, vitality, and creativity (Kohut, 1977). Winnicott (1965, p. 39), sharing that perspective, says flourishing in the period, like so much else, depends on adequate parenting. What he famously called "the good enough mother" quickly intuits and fulfills her baby's needs. When she does so she prompts the baby's formation of the idea of an omnipotent self, the centerpiece of a vital narcissism.

As the baby develops, according to the same view, the mother's responses to the baby naturally slacken, leaving an ever enlarging gap between the baby's desires and their fulfillment. It is as a result of the gap that babies become aware of others' agendas, and their sense of omnipotence gradually and healthily wanes (Winnicott, 1965). But when mothering isn't "good enough," the transition is impeded.[13]

Freud does recognize the value of early narcissism for later growth, contrary to the notion that he denigrates it as something only to be gotten past. The child's mind in general is the wellspring of adult creativity, in the construction of fictional narratives for example (1908a); it is, to Freud, the bedrock of our mental life throughout the lifespan (see Sugarman, 2010). Narcissism in particular, in conjunction with subsequent development, provides the capacity for some experiences such as the susceptibility to the uncanny (Freud, 1919; Sugarman, 2010).

Commentary built on Freud's supposed disregard for the environmental support needed to foster healthy narcissism treats narcissism as an isolated stage he misinterpreted, rather than as the

---

[13]   Practitioners after Freud believed appropriate therapy could play a reparative role in those obstructed situations by providing the responsiveness previously absent in patients' lives; patients would then traverse the developmental stages they missed.

discovery it was. It is an integral constituent of our mental life inferred from a series of observations. Freud noted traits in adults for which he could not account without assuming the existence of a prior developmental stage that made them possible. In that stage the self (ego) becomes the unifying seat of experience, and in that capacity, the self becomes invested with libidinal energy. As a result of the infusion, it forms an inflated idea of itself (Freud, 1914; Chapter 4 here).

Others' commentary, divorced from this theoretical context, cannot address some of the theoretical conundrums to which Freud's account brings order. The conundrums include the parallel between schizophrenic symptoms and manifestations of the "overvaluation" of thought in children – the latter seen, for instance, in children's magical thinking. They also encompass the apparent trade-off between narcissism and object-love; when one intensifies, the other diminishes, suggesting they draw on the same resource – libido – and narcissism is thus a phase of the libido (Freud 1914; Chapter 4 here).[14]

Narcissism as an advance in development

The great Swiss psychologist Jean Piaget questioned Freud's concept of narcissism altogether. He challenged Freud's idea that the telltale signs of children's overvaluation of their mental processes – their magic practices and their superstitious and animistic beliefs, and hence their supposed narcissism – represent an overextended *self*, or ego. He wondered how children could have a sense of self if that self extended without limits; it would just be blurred with everything else.[15] When a child counts to ten between rattles of the radiator to assure the safety of the house at night (magic) or feels sorry for a tree whose middle got hollowed out (animism), she does not know where her own thought and feeling end and the external world begins. She resembles newborn babies who, in their motley sensations, do not

[14] Freud (see Note 5 this chapter) in fact acknowledges the importance of the nurturance of the child generally for the ego's development (e.g., 1910, p. 214), contrary to the representation of his view by later writers (e.g., Fairbairn, 1952; Hartmann, 1939; Spitz, 1965; Winnicott, 1965).

[15] He was not alone in this assessment. See, e.g., Cassirer, 1955; Werner, 1957.

distinguish a self and world; everything is just one stream of experience (Piaget, 1936).

Having stripped Freud's concept of its central ingredient – the ego – Piaget next determined that for an independent self to emerge, children have to disassociate the "indissociated" ideas with which they begin. The requisite radical alteration in their habits of mind comes about, Piaget speculated, through encounters with others, which reinforce children's growing awareness of boundaries between their internal processes and the external world.[16]

Despite its intuitive appeal, Piaget's coupling of the concept of a self with the (correct) knowledge of one's boundaries cannot account for the phenomena it was intended to explain. If children knew no entity "self" and no entity "world," then they could not make the supposed mistakes animism and magic connote. They could not erroneously ascribe what is internal and psychical to what is external and physical, as they do in harboring animistic sentiments, because those discrete categories would not exist for them. In exerting force at a distance in the practice of magic, they would not be mistakenly extending self over a distance, because they would have no self to extend.

Piaget's misreading of Freud's account of narcissism exposes the account's theoretical advantages and also its positive valence. Freud's concept of narcissism avoids the circularity Piaget's formulation generates, because it separates the sense of a self from the question of whether that self draws its boundaries correctly. Although Freud's narcissist misplaces the boundary between self and world, that narcissist does have a unifying seat of experience – what Freud calls the ego, a sense of "I."

The cardinal feature of narcissism is precisely a *self* overextended. That is the concept implied by magic practices and beliefs – which presuppose an "omnipotence of thoughts" (Freud, 1913b, 1919), or an exertion of the self that can have remote effects – and by the

---

[16]   Piaget's conception here is not unlike that of Winnicott's (1965), noted in the last section, in which babies' narcissism begins to wane when they become aware of others' separate agendas.

projection of animistic properties onto the inert. Its megalomanic character is the critical characteristic of schizophrenia and other narcissistic disorders – the original impetus to Freud's delineation of narcissism.

For Freud, narcissism is not part of our original state. It follows the stage of autoeroticism during which we are aroused by diverse stimulation to our bodies, but not by whole objects as such: not other people as unified entities and not a self (Freud, 1914).[17] We might liken that stage, as opposed to Freud's narcissism, to Piaget's undifferentiated, "egocentric" beginning, in which neither self nor world exists and which Piaget intends as our origin.

But now Freud, like Piaget, has to explain how a self would emerge out of the undifferentiated mass of experience with which we begin. Freud's theory proceeds along a track that integrates emotional components with cognitive ones. He says that initially we distinguish what is pleasurable and what is unpleasurable, wanting to retain or repeat pleasurable sensations and dispose of unpleasurable ones (Freud, 1911; Chapter 2 here). Soon we notice that some aversive impressions can be escaped from and some cannot. We begin to separate what is inner and outer on that basis, the inner being inescapable, as hunger pangs are, in that they result from what Freud calls instinct (Freud, 1915a; Chapter 5 here). Although that separation ought to correspond roughly to the objective separation of self and world, Freud says, we quickly distort it. We distort it because we have a tendency to treat the source of any positive experience as part of us – we introject it – and conceive the sources of aversive impressions as alien and outside (Freud, 1915a; Chapter 5, especially note 4, here).[18] That is how the self (ego) comes to have improper boundaries when it does.

---

[17]   Freud's clearest account of the opposition between autoeroticism and narcissism, cited here, may be found in Chapter 3 ("Animism, magic, and the omnipotence of thoughts") of his *Totem and Taboo* (1913b).

[18]   We form that external world in part by "projecting" internally generated discomfort to the outside (Freud, 1913b; Chapter 3 here). What remains inside is thus, as Freud says, pure pleasure-ego (Freud, 1915b; see Chapter 5, note 4 here).

Freud, like Piaget, cannot escape presupposing the existence of the very self he wants to explain, as he does here in imagining that the categories "pleasurable" or "internal" somehow translate to a self. However, what is crucial is that he recognizes a dimension of mental life defined precisely by the condition Piaget would deny – a sense of *self* unaware of its boundaries.[19]

Narcissism and agency

Freud's psychoanalytic successors see in that attainment of omnipotence something to celebrate and cultivate, not to disparage or to impede. But Freud, contrasting that omnipotence with the previous egoless state of autoeroticism, uncovers something more elemental – something his successors, in their readiness to capture his denigration of the infantile, seem to have overlooked. It is that narcissism, realized as the self overextended, asserts "*I*" caused this. Even if "I" didn't do it from the external observer's perspective, "I" exists and has agency.

FREUD'S THEORY: A CONSOLIDATION

In his search for the most basic principles of mental life, Freud at the end of his career reached all the way back to the beginning of life. There he identified, respectively, an impulsion toward life and a drift toward quiescence, ultimately death, or inorganicity.

Likewise, the individual mind strives toward the clamor of life and its tensions, on the one hand, and the release from tension and stimulus, on the other, the latter expressed by and originating in the reflex. The search for pleasure and retreat from pain – the "pleasure principle" – which Freud takes as a psychological primitive, converges in part with that division: the striving for pleasure may incorporate both the attempt to reduce stimulus and the pursuit of it, while the attempt to avoid pain, or unpleasure, expresses the drift toward quiescence. Historically, we needed to make sure our pleasures were real, as

---

[19]   Piaget does manage to slip in a concept of inflated self as well as the idea of undifferentiated self and world, but the idea is unmotivated in the theory (see Sugarman, 1987).

opposed to illusory, and to adjust our aims in that light; as we move forward we likewise need to monitor possible consequences of our intended actions and again modify our aims accordingly.

The life and death instincts almost always intermix. Aggression is a prime example of their combination. For, Freud theorizes, we are born with a death instinct directed inward in the form of a trend toward decomposition. On account of the intervention of the life instincts, the trend is directed outward where it assumes the active form of destruction upon the world. By now in our evolution, aggression forms copiously and instantaneously enough that Freud conceives it as a free-standing instinct in its own right.

Within the envelope of the life and death instincts and the pursuit of pleasure fit the day-to-day needs we satisfy, which Freud characterized as concerned most broadly with, respectively, sexual life and the preservation of self, or ego. The sexual instincts form around the prototype of reproduction, which produces new life and translates into various needs both closely and only distantly related to that function; sexual foreplay and intercourse would be closely, and thumb-sucking and the pleasure of touch distantly, related. Erotic ties and friendship also form part of the sexual instinct. The ego instincts see to our individual survival. Both groups of needs set the pleasure principle in motion. When we have the need, say, of hunger, pain and tension arise and ease only when the need achieves satisfaction.

Through various mechanisms Freud describes, our strivings complicate well beyond these basal impulses. They undergo "vicissitudes," changes in their direction, aim, or vehicle of satisfaction, the vicissitudes initially brought about by an actual or anticipated obstacle to their fulfillment.

Freud's final taxonomy for distinguishing different interests and methods of operation within the mind includes an id, ego, and superego. The "id" signifies pure impulse absent any judgment or reflection. We wish, or want, only. The thinking self as we know it is embodied by the ego, which, in addition to wishing and wanting, judges, reasons, and monitors our navigation of the external world.

The superego, built up from our internalization of our parents, appraises the actions of the self, often harshly.

Our ongoing behavior is the result of the joint action of all these strands of mentation. Rarely in our conscious waking life do we operate on pure impulse; we engage in thought and reflection too, judging and making choices. At the same time, we rarely know all the motivations of our impulses. They are, as Freud would say, over-determined, with some of those influences inaccessible to consciousness. For instance, we might not know why, or fully why, we want or like something or where a given thought came from.

When the different interests within our minds converge, or when, in competition, they are able variously to achieve at least partial expression, we enjoy a state of psychological health.[20] But it is inherent to human experience that that convergence occurs only some of the time. At other times the interests of id and ego or superego may conflict. For example, a lustful or hostile urge (id) and a sense of propriety (superego) may conflict and lead us to recognize either external or internal repercussions we cannot abide (ego); conflicts within the ego may arise as well.[21] When the poles of the conflict are unconscious, we can do little consciously to either unearth or ameliorate the conflict. Symptoms may erupt when the conflict becomes stronger than we can contain, though in doing so they can also, as just noted, provide clues to their source. Who will fall ill is complexly determined; Freud knows only that experience and constitution both play a role, such that, for example, of two people with the same life experience only one might develop a neurosis.

[20] Recall, regarding psychological health, Freud's depiction of "energetic and successful" people as those who find a way to realize their wishful fantasies in reality (Freud, 1909a, p. 50; Chapter 1 here)

[21] Freud emphasizes the possibility of "splitting" within the ego in his final works, *An Outline of Psychoanalysis* (1940a, Chapter VIII) and "The splitting of the ego in the processes of defense" (1940b). Although he originally formed the idea with reference to cases of fetishism (Freud, 1927b), he eventually recognized its applicability to any instance in which the ego needs to erect a defense, regardless of whether the offending impulse originates in the ego or elsewhere, for example in the id.

Our behavior, in both illness and health, is the result not only of the interacting forces within our minds and the experiences upon which those forces play, but also of the development of the mind. As we grow older and our minds become capable of repression, they become a repository for impulses and impressions pushed from consciousness but not forgotten, in consequence of which they remain active. The action of the repository results in behavior whose source(s) become ever more difficult to detect. Pathology, along with the complex emotions of shame and disgust, for example, forms from the sequelae of repression.

Development produces other changes, beside the separation of conscious and unconscious. We naturally surmount primitive viewpoints and modes of thought, for example the ego-centeredness, overvaluation of thought, and animism of our early narcissism: we outgrow at least some of our sense of omnipotence and regularly observe the boundary between animate and inanimate (Freud, 1919). We learn decorum (Freud, 1908a): we reflect, judge, and restrain ourselves, where we might have acted impulsively before. These new capabilities, more than simply overtaking their predecessors, may occasionally intermix with them, allowing, according to Freud, complex aesthetic experiences, like the susceptibility to the uncanny (Freud, 1919) and the appreciation and production of the comic (Freud, 1905b).

It is perhaps in the delineation of the superego that Freud delivers his most complex vision of development and its impact on our mental life. The idea of a superego establishes the mind as more than its urges and passions – the id – and more than the thought and calculations that enable our everyday doings and the curbing of the passions – the ego. We also, in the light of the interests Freud calls superego, filter everything we do, think, and feel through a lens of self-appraisal.

Not least among those outcomes is our moral sensibility. The imperative we feel when we think it morally right or morally wrong to do something exceeds mere knowledge of moral rules and the expectation of negative repercussions should we violate them. It reflects the legacy that gives us the superego: the love, animosity, and urgency we experienced at our parents' knees; the further hostility we turned back upon ourselves for fear of abandonment by them; the introjection of them that followed upon our relinquishment of ambitions for total possession of them. We are moral not because we are innately endowed for it or because we learn to be so, but because we follow an inner compulsion that arises as a byproduct of our early emotional life and our inexorable development past it.

Freud, though read as having emphasized our origins and basal principles at the expense of capturing our full humanity, searched persistently for those origins and principles to extrapolate to the forces that move us beyond them. His theory is no more reductionist for that attempt than is geometry in its use of axioms to anchor extended chains of reasoning. To grasp the theory, we need to see its touchstones as the start of a chain of reasoning and not the end of one.

References

In this book, the abbreviation *SE* has been used for *The Standard Edition of the Complete Psychological Works of Sigmund Freud*, J. Strachey, Trans. and General Ed. London: Hogarth, 1981.

Alexander, F. (1927). *The Psychoanalysis of the Total Personality*, B. Glueck and B.D. Lewin, Trans. New York: Nervous and Mental Disease Publishers, 1930.

Beigel, H.G. (1953). Sex and human beauty. *Journal of Aesthetics and Art Criticism*, 12 (1), 83–92.

Bion, W.R. (1984). *Learning from Experience*. London: Karnac Books. Originally published 1962.

Bowlby, J. (1969). *Attachment and Loss: Vol. 1. Attachment*. New York: Basic.

Breuer, J., & Freud, S. (1893–1895). *Studies in Hysteria, SE, II*.

Cassirer, E. (1955). *The Philosophy of Symbolic Forms: Vol. 2, Mythical Thought*. New Haven, CT: Yale University Press.

Darwin, C. (1871). *The Descent of Man, and Selection in Relation to Sex*. London: J. Murray.

Dyster-Aas, J., Arnberg, F.K., Lindam, A., Johannesson, K. B., Lundin, T., Michel, P.-O. (2012). Impact of phsycial injury on mental health after the 2004 Southest Asia tsunami. *Nordic Journal of Psychiatry*, 66, 203–208.

Erikson, E. (1950). *Childhood and Society*. New York: Norton.

(1958). *Young Man Luther*. New York: Norton.

Fairbairn, W.R.D. (1952). *An Object Relations Theory of the Personality*. New York: Basic.

(1994). *From Instinct to Self: Selected Papers of W.R.D. Fairbairn* (Vols. 1–2) (E. F. Birtles & D.E. Scharff, Eds.). Northvale, NJ: Jason Aronson.

Fechner, G.T. (1873). *Einige Ideen zur Schöpfungs- und Entwickelungsgeschichte der Organismen*. Leipzig: Druck und verlag von Breitkopf und Haertel.

Ferenczi, S. (1909). Introjection and transference, *Contributions to Psychoanalysis*, E. Jones (Trans.), Toronto: Richard G. Badger, pp. 30–79.

Frazer, J.G. (1911a). *The Magic Art* (2 vols.)(*The Golden Bough*, Third Edition, Part I). London: Macmillan.

(1911b). *Totem and the Perils of the Soul* (The Golden Bough, Third Edition, Part I). London: Macmillan.

Freud, S. (1895). Project for a scientific psychology. *SE, I,* 283–397.

(1900). *The Interpretation of Dreams. SE, IV–V.*

(1901). *The Psychopathology of Everyday Life. SE, VI.*

(1905a). *Three essays on the theory of sexuality. SE, VII,* 125–246.

(1905b). *Jokes and their relation to the unconscious. SE, VIII.*

(1908a). Creative writers and daydreaming. *SE, IX,* 141–153.

(1908b). 'Civilized' sexual morality and modern nervous illness. *SE, IX,* 177–204.

(1909a). *Five Lectures on Psychoanalysis. SE, XI,* 3–56.

(1909b). Analysis of a phobia in a five-year-old boy. *SE, X,* 1–149.

(1909c). Notes upon a case of obsessional neurosis. *SE, X,* 153–318.

(1910). Leonardo da Vinci and a memory of his childhood. *SE, XI,* 59–136.

(1911). Formulations regarding two principles in mental functioning. *SE, XII,* 213–226.

(1913a). The disposition to obsessional neurosis. *SE, XII,* 311–326.

(1913b). *Totem and Taboo. SE, XIII,* ix–162.

(1914). On narcissism: an introduction. *SE, XIV,* 67–102.

(1915a). Instincts and their vicissitudes. *SE, XIV,* 109–140.

(1915b). Repression. *SE, XIV,* 139–158.

(1915c). The unconscious. *SE, XIV,* 159–215.

(1916). Some character types met with in psychoanalytic work. *SE, XIV,* 309–333.

(1917a). *Introductory Lectures on Psychoanalysis,* Part III. *SE,* XVI.

(1917b). A difficulty in the path of psychoanalysis. *SE, XVII,* 135–144.

(1917c). Mourning and melancholia. *SE, XIV,* 237–260.

(1918). From the history of an infantile neurosis. *SE,* 1–123.

(1919). The 'uncanny'. *SE, VII,* 217–256.

(1920). *Beyond the Pleasure Principle. SE, XVIII,* 3–64.

(1921). *Group Psychology and the Analysis of the Ego. SE, XVIII,* 65–143.

(1923). *The Ego and the Id. SE, XIX,* 3–66.

(1924). The economic problem in masochism. *SE, XIX,* 157–170.

(1925a). Negation. *SE, XIX,* 233–239.

(1925b). An autobiographical study. *SE, XX,* 1–74.

(1925c). A note upon the 'Mystic Writing-Pad.' *SE, XIX,* 225–232.

(1926). *Inhibitions, Symptoms, and Anxiety. SE, XX,* 77–181.

(1927a). *The Future of an Illusion. SE, XXI,* 1–56.

(1927b). Fetishism. *SE, XXI,* 147–157.

(1930). Civilization and its Discontents, *SE, XXI,* 57–145.

(1936). A disturbance of memory on the Acropolis: An open letter to Romain Rolland on the occasion of his seventieth birthday. *SE, XXII*, 239–248.

(1937). Letter #33 to Marie Bonaparte. In E. Jones, *The life and work of Sigmund Freud, Vol. 3*. New York: Basic, 1957, 464–465.

(1939). *Moses and Monotheism. SE, XXIII*, 1–137.

(1940a). *An Outline of Psychoanalysis. SE, XXIII*, 141–207.

(1940b). The splitting of the ego in the processes of defense. *SE, XXIII*, 271–278.

Govrin, A. (2004). Some utilitarian influences in Freud's early writings. *Psychoanalysis and History*, 6, 5–21.

Groddeck, G. (1923). *Book of the It*. (V.M.E. Collins, trans.) New York: Funk and Wagnalls, 1950.

Hartmann, H. (1939). *Ego Psychology and the Problem of Adaptation* (David Rappaport, trans.) New York: International Universities Press.

Hering, E. (1878). *Zur Lehre vom Lichtsinne*. Vienna.

Jacobson, E. (1964). *The Self and the Object World*. New York: International Universities Press.

Jones. E. (1957). *The Life and Work of Sigmund Freud*, Vol. 1. New York: Basic.

Kaempfer, E. (1727). *The History of Japan* (2 vols.), London.

Kernberg, O. (1976). *Object Relations Theory and Clinical Psychoanalysis*. New York: Jason Aronson.

Klein, M. (1957). *Envy and Gratitude and Other Works: 1946–1963*. New York: Delacorte, 1975.

Kohut, H. (1977). *The Restoration of the Self*. New York: International Universities Press.

(1979). The two analyses of Mr. Z. *International Journal of Psychoanalysis*, 60, 3–27. Reprinted in H. Kohut (1991), *The Search for the Self, IV*. Madison, CT: International Universities Press, 395–446.

(1984). *How Does Analysis Cure?* Chicago: University of Chicago Press.

Koren, D., Norman, D., Cohen, A., Berman, J., Klein, E.M. (2005). Increased PTSD risk with combat-related injury: A matched comparison study of injured and uninjured soldiers experiencing the same combat events. *American Journal of Psychiatry*, 162, 276–282.

Lear, J. (2000). *Happiness, Death, and the Remainder of Life*. Cambridge, MA: Harvard.

(2005). *Freud*. Abingdon: Routledge.

Lipschütz, A. (1914). *Warum wir sterben*. Stuttgart.

Loewald, H. (1988). *Sublimation*. New Haven: Yale.

Low, B. (1920). *Psychoanalysis: A Brief Account of the Freudian Theory*. New York: Harcourt-Brace.

Mahler, M. (1968). *On Human Symbiosis and the Vicissitudes of Individuation*. [Vol. 1. *Infantile Psychosis*.] New York: International Universities Press.

McIsaac, R.S., Huang, K.C., Sengupta, A., and Wingreen, N.S. (2011). Does the potential for chaos constrain the embryonic cell-cycle oscillator? *PLOS/Computational Biology*. http://www.ploscompbiol.org/article/info%3Ado i%2F10.1371%2Fjournal.pcbi.1002109.

Mitchell, S.A., and Black, M.J. (1995). *Freud and Beyond: A History of Psychoanalytic Thought*. New York: Basic.

Piaget, J. (1936). *The Origins of Intelligence in Children*. (M. Cook, trans.) New York: International Universities Press, 1952.

Schafer, R.S. (1976). *A New Language for Psychoanalysis*. New Haven: Yale University Press.

Schaffer, H.R. & Emerson, P.E. (1964). The development of social attachment in infancy. *Monographs of the Society for Research in Child Development*, 29, no.3, serial no.94.

Sijbrandij, M., Engelhard, I.M., de Vries, G-J, Luitse, J.S.K., Carlier, I.V.E., Gersons, B.P.R., Olff, M. (2013). The role of injury and trauma-related variables in the onset and course of symptoms of posttraumatic stress disorder. *Journal of Clinical Psychology in Medical Settings*, 20, 449–455.

Spitz, R.A. (1965). (in collaboration with W.G. Cobliner) *The First Year of Life: A Psychoanalytic Study of Normal and Deviant Development of Object Relations*. New York: International Universities Press.

Stern, D.B. (1985). *The Interpersonal World of the Infant: A View from Psychoanalysis and Developmental Psychology*. New York: Basic Books.

Strachey, J. (1957). Editorial note to S. Freud, "Repression" (1915/1957), *SE, XIV*, pp. 143–145.

Sugarman, S. (1987). *Piaget's Construction of the Child's Reality*. New York: Cambridge.

(2010). *Freud on the Psychology of Ordinary Mental Life*. New York: Rowman-Littlefield.

Weismann, A. (1884). *Über Leben und Tod*. Jena.

Werner, H. (1957). *A Comparative Psychology of Mental Development*. New York: International Universities Press.

Winnicott, D.W. (1965). *The Maturational Processes and the facilitating Environment: Studies in the Theory of Emotional Development*. Madison, CT: International Universities Press (Ch. 1, p. 19, MB 133).

Woodruff, L.L. (1914). A five-year pedigreed race of *Paramecium* without conjugation. *Proceedings of the Society for Experimental Biology*, 9.

Wundt., W. (1906). *Mythus und Religion*, Teil II *Völkerpsychologie*, Lepzig: W. Englemann.

Index

Action, voluntary, 20, 114
Active–passive reversal of instincts. *See*
        Vicissitudes of instincts: reversal
        into the opposite: active–passive
Aesthetic activity/appreciation. *See* Art;
        Beauty; Theatrical display
Affect. *See* Emotion
Afterlife. *See* Religion: afterlife in
Agency
    loss of alleged of id, ego, superego
        scheme, 150, 167
    narcissism embodying, 173
    psychoanalytic therapy, encouraged
        by, 167
Aggression
    civilization, threat to, 130, 137, 140
    death instinct
        derived from, 103, 130, 139
        distinct from, 103
        diversion of, 102, 174
    free-standing inclination, 140, 164
    guilt
        consequence of checking, 118–119,
            127, 128, 141, 145
        proportional to checking, 142
    identification as antidote to, 137
    instincts theory of, place within,
        138–141, 164
    instinctual fusion, instance of, 112
    life and death instincts, derivative of,
        103, 112, 139–140, 164, 174
    masochism, and, 128
    universal love as antidote to, 136–137
Ambivalence
    guilt, source of, 145
    love and hate, in, 56, 59–61
    obsessional neurosis, in, 29–31
    primal horde, in, 144–145
    relationships, characteristic of, 34
    taboo, in, 27
    vicissitudes of instincts, inherent in, 55–56

Anal–sadistic sexual organization/anal
        eroticism, 10, 133, 161
Animals, nonhuman
    attachment theory and, 157
    civilization and, 133
    higher development, absence of instinct
        toward, 98
    human mental life traceable to, 157, 159
    id, ego, and superego in, 111–112
    life and death instincts, absence of
        struggle between in, 141
Animism, 170, 171
Anna O. (case history), 5, 6, 7, 8, 66, 68, 75, 81,
        85, 118
Anticathexis, 79, *See also* Energy, psychic
Anxiety
    birth experience source of manifestations
        of, 119
    birth, occasioned by. *See* Birth anxiety
    buffer against trauma, 93
    castration, regarding. *See* Castration
        anxiety
    ego seat of, 119
    fear of death as species of, 120
    fright, contrast with, 93
    repressed affects and, 65
    separation, stemming from. *See*
        Separation anxiety
    social. *See* Social anxiety
    superego/conscience generation of,
        119–120
Anxiety hysteria. *See* Hysteria: anxiety
Art, 12, 13, 24–25, 131, 133, 134
Attachment, theory of, 157
Attention, origin of, 20
Autoeroticism, 10, 22, 23, 39, 55, 172, 173

Beauty, enjoyment of, 131, 133, 161
Binding
    communities, 21, 136
    death instinct, 124